T0090674

Homesteading on the Dry Fork of the Marias River

The Legacy of LaVern and Vivian Keil

Homesteading on the Dry Fork of the Marias River

Homesteading on the Dry Fork of the Marias River

The Legacy of LaVern and Vivian Keil

Oral and written story by
Vivian Venetz Keil

Edited by
Christine Frankland
Loretta Grubb
Charlotte Marshall
Gwen Marshall

Layout, design, & typesetting by
Christine Frankland

Order this book online at www.trafford.com
or email orders@trafford.com

Most Trafford titles are also available at major online book retailers.

© Copyright 2010 Vivan Venetz Keil.
All rights reserved. No part of this publication may be reproduced, stored in a retrieval system,
or transmitted, in any form or by any means, electronic, mechanical, photocopying, recording,
or otherwise, without the written prior permission of the author.

The views expressed in this work are solely those of the author and do not necessarily reflect the
views of the publisher, and the publisher hereby disclaims any responsibility for them.

Printed in the United States of America.

ISBN: 978-1-4269-4205-1 (sc)

*Our mission is to efficiently provide the world's finest, most comprehensive book publishing
service, enabling every author to experience success. To find out how to publish your book,
your way, and have it available worldwide, visit us online at www.trafford.com*

Trafford rev. 09/28/2010

 www.trafford.com

North America & international
toll-free: 1 888 232 4444 (USA & Canada)
phone: 250 383 6864 ♦ fax: 812 355 4082

Book Dedication

To my best friend and husband LaVern Keil and to my family.

July 1985, 50th wedding anniversary, Conrad Legion Park. Front row (left to right): Jay Grubb, Wade Hawley, Helen Keil Hawley, Gwen Marshall, Chris, Jennifer, Jeremy Danbrook. Middle row: Ross & Jill Grubb, Devra Grubb, Terri Prewett, Charlotte Marshall, LaVern, Vivian, Sherri Keil, Loretta Grubb, Louella Keil, Jenniffer, baby Calvin, & Rollie Schlepp. Back row: Mark & baby Kristi Grubb, Randy Prewett, Bob Marshall, Kent, Brent & Dale Keil, Erling Grubb, & Don Keil.

Front Cover Photo: The Dry Fork, Burlington Sante Fe Railroad

Back Cover Photo: LaVern and Vivian's 50th anniversary

Preface

Reader you are in for an amazing oral history by me, Vivian Keil of the living and shaping of a Montana farm and ranch family. The history spans the 1700s to current family history and trials of LaVern and my families trek from Europe to the present in Montana. The family history has been traced as far as written records have allowed, following the ancestral farmers migrating from Germany to Russia to America, and Switzerland to America. An in-depth history of the family in Montana begins in the first half of the 1900's and discusses the trial and tribulations of farming and ranching above the Dry Fork of the Marias River in Montana. The hardships of homesteading, surviving the depression, living through the dust storms, and adaptations these rugged pioneers had to make to survive. The marvel of their undaunted courage to move to the unfamiliar, start with little, and persevere in a rugged country is amazing to say the least.

LaVern and I loved the land and the ranch. We farmed, leveled land, built roads, raised registered grain, helped develop and increase new barleys and other crops and did lots of fencing. We implemented alkali control practices and planted shelterbelts. Above all, we loved our cattle. We had no hobbies; our life was the farm and ranch.

LaVern was very generous to those in need. Reverend McCorkle used to stop by with stories of the needs of the neediest such as orphans; Boulder special needs institution in Boulder, Montana, and reform schools. We always gave to support those in need. If folks could not pay for a funeral or food or other unexpected expenses, we would always help out.

We were involved in many conservation programs, were very active in the running of, and participated in the Ledger Community Hall activities, including serving on the board of directors.

Join us in the journey of our ancestors and the hardships endured during the settling of the expanding west. The story of individuals and families who immigrated to a foreign land with the promise of land. The trials and tribulations of establishing farms and ranches during the turn of the century, and the continuation and improvement of those endeavors throughout the generations.

Table of Contents

Chapter 1
LaVern's family history

Germany to Russia to the United States:

Marie Katherine Keil (nee) Heinitz was born March 4, 1822 at Werchnaja Kulalinka, Russia an area near the Volga River. Marie was confirmed in the church in 1838 in Nstkulalinka, Russia. She married John Reinhardt Keil's father, Adam. She had four sons. John George Keil, a stepson was born February 15, 1842. John Frederick Keil was born January 4, 1855. John Conrad Keil was born July 12, 1863. John Reinhardt Keil was born June 28, 1865 at Eckholm, Russia and later baptized on August 20, 1865. Marie was widowed in 1869.

The above record was taken from a paper brought by Marie Katherine when she migrated to the United States in 1877 with her boys, along with other colonists to avoid militarism. The parents of these same colonists had migrated to Russia from Germany during the reign of Catharine II also to avoid militarism somewhere between 1762 and 1796. Proud of their German heritage, language and customs, they retained them by living in colonies and not mixing with the Russians.

John Reinhardt Keil: Lavern's fraternal grandfather:

Reinhardt's boyhood memories of his life in Russia include not only his disdain for the natives, but the beauty of the countryside, which was covered with wild flowers.

Upon arrival in America, the large group was kept together first at Ellis Island and later at Fort Leavenworth until a large enough tract of land could be found on which these farmers could settle. They finally settled in Russell County, Kansas near Milberger where Reinhardt was married to Mollie Bauer and engaged in farming. Mollie had come to America with the Kinsvather family from Freidenfold, Russia. She was

Molly Bauer Keil

a young woman and promised to an older Foos boy. Hannah, Mollie's first child later married a younger Foos boy, Philip.

There was a rumor of vast expansion in North Dakota and Canada, so with his fast growing family, in a covered wagon, Reinhardt explored these regions during the year. He stayed in Grand Forks, North Dakota long enough to build a house. Not finding what he was looking for, he returned to Kansas settling first near Hill City and then on the old Timken ranch. They had eight children; Hannah, John, Jake, Elma, Amelia, George, Leslie, and Laura. After Mollie's death when George, the baby, was four months old and the ranch broke up into smaller units, he moved near Rozell, Kansas.

For two years following his wife's death, he struggled to keep a home for his family. George was living with the Kinsvather family and Elma with the George and Fred Keil families. Reinhardt heard of a widow living in Great Bend with seven children, whom he had known in his youth, who was also in desperate straits. Daring to face the scorn of his fellow German neighbors, he married the American woman, Hattie Harminson Butler and became the father of her children who all grew to love and respect him. Showing no favoritism between his and her children, he was known for his ability to hold the family together. He was a keen student of the Bible and nearly all arguments were settled by a quotation from it. He and his three sons, Henry, Jake and August, were well known for their music on the violin, piano, dulcimer and auto harp for home entertainments, dances and weddings. These three boys later moved to Montana with their families. After a year at Elkhart, Kansas, Reinhardt took what was left of his family, two more had been added, Alice and Ida, and moved to Montana where during the latter part of his life, dry years came and there were hard times throughout the nation.

He was driving a truck for LaVern, who was putting out posts for a fence. He began driving erratically and LaVern knew something was wrong. He took grandpa back to Fowler where he was living at the time. Suffering a stroke of cerebral hemorrhage, he died December 19, 1934 at Conrad, Montana.

The sequel to Reinhardt Keil as told by Henry Keil follows:

When Reinhardt and Mollie Bauer were first married, they lived with his brother or at the family home of his grandmother. There was Fred Sr. and a wife, Reinhardt's brother, Fred Jr. and wife, and Reinhardt, wife and family all in one home and working together for several years, until conditions enabled them to branch out independently. When their first baby was coming, Reinhardt went to

Mollie Bauer Keil and brother-in-law Fred Keil

an elderly midwife and studied and trained for the event. There was no doctor near and no other means of delivering babies except by midwife. He had been engaged to furnish music for a New Year's Eve celebration when he was told that Mollie, his wife, was in labor. He dropped everything, put aside his violin, went home and delivered the baby, attended to all of the medical needs and even dressed the child. When Mollie was safe and secure, he returned to the New Year's Eve celebration in time to play the "Home Sweet Home" waltz.

Reinhardt was a very thoughtful person and was forever helping someone less fortunate than himself. In times of drought, he would remark, "Those folks really do need a rain," etc., never saying "I" or "we" need the rain. They moved to a farm east of Russell, Kansas for a couple of years where Henry, August and Jake were born. Later they moved out to Bison close to the Kinsvathers; Auntie Kinsvather was Mollie's sister.

The following is a family story as passed down through the generations. The authenticity is not known, but it sure made for an interesting story. Uncle Kinsvather was quite a horse fancier. He always had good-blooded horses and raised several very famous ones in his time. All the girls, even to Hannah, would help exercise and practice the horses. He purchased a blooded mare and her colt to train. A very short time later, a horseman from the east came through. He stopped at Hays City, and saw this colt work. Knowing he had to have him, he finally made a deal with Uncle Kinsvather at what was then an enormous price. He took the colt back East, and called him Dan Patch, and he became internationally famous as a pacer.

After John was born, they moved to Hill City or Graham County where Emelia and Elma were born. There things were not very fruitful, except babies, and Reinhardt and another family (Mr. Schwein) loaded up their families in covered wagons and leading extra horses behind, headed for the North Country. It was the middle of February and Elma was only six weeks old. They got to Grand Island, Nebraska, in early March after a cold, tough winter, and everyone was tired. So, they decided to ship via immigrant train the rest of the way. They loaded the two wagons and six horses in an immigrant car and Mr. Schwein took charge of the car, while Reinhardt stowed away. The women and children would go via passenger train. Henry, who was a year or two, too old to have a free ride, was out with some of the other boys his age playing games. He did not know or understand

Family on a trip

just what was going on when they picked him up, rushed him down to the train and hid him in the car with his father and took off. It stayed with him all these years that he was compelled to leave and hide out like that without bidding his mother and the other kid's good-bye. He was sure he would never see them again.

This being in the winter, Reinhardt and Henry kept warm in feather ticks and they ate crackers, cheese, sausage, etc., replenishing their food supplies when the train stopped. They always had to fill the water barrels in the stock cars, so the cattle and horses could have water. The stock stayed in the rail cars the entire trip. The brakeman discovered them and told them not to smuggle themselves across the border into Canada, but to declare themselves, which they did.

When they arrived in Winnipeg, Canada, and all found each other, they were at an immigrant house. All the farms or homesteads and everything were under water from the melting winter snow. While out trying to find a place to live, Reinhardt nearly lost his horses and himself in the icy water while crossing a stream full of floating ice. He jumped out of his wagon in waist-deep water to save his horses. He became very ill the next day and was forced to turn back towards Kansas. When he was well enough, they loaded up and drove back to Grand Forks where they stayed for some time. Children added to the food supply by gathering flowers from along the roadside, and selling them in saloons in order to buy milk. In Grand Forks, they lived in a house with a low-ceilinged attic where some of the children slept. Mollie was expecting another baby and while cleaning or rearranging, raised up to a standing position, struck the top of her head on the roof beam above, and passed out. She was sick for several weeks, causing her to lose that baby. Reinhardt was very sad, and felt that that was the cause of the illness that would occur with each childbirth. Mollie never recovered following George's birth and passed away on September 25, 1906, at Osawatomie, Kansas.

When they left Grand Forks for Kansas, Reinhardt had sold his house, purchased a high-spirited team of horses, and had only $35.00 in his possession. They had to take turns driving the horses, as they were the kind that was pulling on their bits all day long. Hannah, a young girl and fond of driving, would take her turn, but would soon tire, start to cry, and Reinhardt would take the lines again. While camping on an Indian Reservation, where they had to cross the Missouri River on a ferryboat, they contracted fleas. There were fleas in their food, fleas in their clothing, and fleas in their beds. It took them several days to rid themselves of the pests. After they were safely away from flea country, they would get out of the wagon and run along the roadside. Going through the country, they would locate prairie chicken nests and gather the eggs that were still fresh, and have them to make potato dumplings. Mollie would mix up the dough and set the bread. On the move, when the bread was ready to put in the bake pans, they would watch for a farmhouse, stop and ask to use the oven. They were never turned down in the six weeks it took to make the trip. A lone cowboy happened along and helped with the reading of a rough map they had of the area. Henry had put pins in the map to signify certain places. Reinhardt was very grateful. Kindly Mennonites invited them to stay and rest for a couple of days, and even offered to lend them money, they stayed but Reinhardt refused the money.

After Mollies death, Reinhardt was lost, confused and bewildered. He set up housekeeping with the boys on the farm they had rented at Rozell, Kansas. He rounded up several violins and the auto harp and started the boys on musical sessions, which became so familiar and appreciated by everyone within calling distance. The boys were pretty good cooks, too, in time. Some kind neighbor women would come in and show them how to make bread and biscuits. They even attempted cake baking.

Hattie Sophia Harmison; LaVern's maternal grandmother:
As told by Clara Butler Grigsby

Hattie was born in Bloomington, Illinois. Her parents lived on a small farm where they raised corn and sugar cane.

In 1871, the family decided to go out West where they could file on 160 acres of farmland. They had two children, Nellie and Hattie ages 2 and 4, and the third child, William was born in the covered wagon on their way west.

They settled on a homestead near what is now the city of Wichita, Kansas and began the uphill fight of making a home in that as yet unsettled territory.

Food was indeed scarce and when cool weather came in the fall, the men of the settlement would hitch their teams to wagons and go on farther west where buffalo herds still roamed and they would kill enough of the beasts for their winter meat.

Their hardships were very great. It was 80 miles to the nearest railroad and there was very little money locally to purchase the small amount of crop they were able to produce.

Prairie fires were an ever present and deadly menace. Mother told me of one in particular. Her mother was going to help with some task in the field the next day, so a neighbor lady volunteered to take the baby home with her. They were just about half a mile from the house when they were horrified to see a prairie fire approaching with express train speed. I'm sure that any of you who have ever lived in Kansas know what I mean; with dry prairie grass and a high wind, all one could do was watch. There was an adequate fireguard (cleared area) around the sod house so the rest of them watched in horror as the smoke and flames hid the neighbor woman and the baby from sight.

As soon as the fire had passed, Grandpa jumped on a horse and quickly rode to the place where they had last seen the woman and the baby, but could see no sign of them. He was amazed to hear someone call and began looking around and found them in an abandoned well about eight feet deep, which the lady had been lucky

Row crop tractor.

Single cylinder gas engine (big radiator on front) for powering the threshing machine. It is being moved with a smaller Case tractor.

enough to spot in the nick of time.

They stayed long enough to prove up on the homestead, then feeling that they had had their fill of the Wild West; they sold it for enough to get back to Illinois. This was in 1874 when mother was five years old. This time they moved to Urbana, Illinois, where they lived a short ways out of town on a small farm. To make a little extra, Grandpa operated a custom sorghum mill.

But the call of the West was too strong and again in 1878 Grandpa headed west. He was sure that this time he could find a place where he could build a home for his fast growing family; by this time, there were five children. The

Steam engine powering the thresing machine. Threshing from a bundle stack.

Horse drawn wagons moved the corn harvest crop in Kansas.

Union Pacific had built a railroad across Kansas and much of Illinois was getting too crowded. They would have to go West of Kansas.

This time he went alone to locate a place to settle and then send for his family. He arrived at what is known as the old coal bank on the Smokey River with $.25 in his pocket and a barrel of sorghum molasses in the wagon. It was never been quite clear to me how or why he happened to have the sorghum along, but at any rate, he was able to trade a few gallons at a time for horse feed and food for himself until he was able to find some sort of work.

Having already used his homestead rights, he was able to procure 160 acres of school land and 160 acres additional, which was called a timber claim. This land was located about five miles northeast of Galatia, Kansas and about the same distance from Milberger where just one year earlier a colony of immigrants from Russia had settled, and Reinhardt Keil was one of them.

With the help of other settlers who were always glad to see new people move in; a one-room sod house was quickly built, a well dug and the family sent for. They arrived in grand style by train in Russell the spring of 1879.

There were, of course, no schools and no public monies available or ever heard of, so the settlers selected a centrally located spot. The settlers broke sod and built a sod school of sorts. There being no material for a floor, the ground itself served the purpose. Crude benches were fashioned out of any material that could be found. Everyone dug up all school material that could be found. Everyone dug up old school books they had brought with them from wherever they had come and a collection was taken to pay a teacher. They raised $60 and with that, and they were able to hire a local woman, who had completed grade school to teach a three-month term. Incidentally, she walked the five miles to and from the school, daily.

The year of 1880 was a year of drought and they were unable to raise enough money for one month, much less, three months to pay the teacher. So there was no school except for what the mothers were able to teach their children at home. They were able to have another three-month term in the fall of 1881. By 1882, public money was made available and they were able to have regular six-month terms from then on but the families took turns boarding the teacher.

The sod schoolhouse served as a church as well as a recreation center. A minister who lived about 40 miles away was able to get there for services about once a month and he was a healer of the body as well as the soul.

Mother remembers that a cat had scratched Aunt Mary's nose and it was badly infected, as it was all red and swollen. The minister healed it with his cure-all salve; it was a camphor gum the size of a thimble, beeswax the size of a hulled walnut and ½ cup of lard.

The men folk of the settlement, using shovels and homemade scrapers, cleared the grass and leveled a large enough space in the schoolyard where croquet parties were held.

Other forms of recreation were taffy pulls, old-fashioned party games such as *Skip to My Lou*, *Miller Boy* and yes, you guessed it, *Post Office*. There were also quilting parties and carpet tacking. I had never heard of this before so I asked just what it was. The answer: everyone who wanted a rag carpet brought their carpet rags to one place and all joined in together to sew them so the rags were ready to be woven. When they were all sewn together, the woman would serve a huge potluck meal and party games or dancing would follow.

The recreation, which assumed the greatest importance, was the literary or debate society. Their subjects for debate ranged from the sublime to the ridiculous, but always attracted people from as far away as 10 or even 15 miles. These individuals would come to hear the local orators expound.

In 1881, the men folk of the settlement were offered work on the railroad in Colorado. So they would ship their horses out there to help build railroad. One of Grandpa Harmison's horses took pneumonia and died enroute which was a near tragedy as it cost the amazing sum of $60 to replace it before he could start work.

In the fall of this same year, the wild geese came in such numbers that they ate all the grain in the fields. They were so full of corn they were unable to rise and fly, so they were killed without using any ammunition and were canned up for food.

In 1882, Grandpa wrote to his father and had the sorghum mill sent out. He let people know it was coming so he had plenty of customers that fall. People came from many miles to have their sugar cane made into sorghum.

Building a bundle stack. Note the extra side boards on the bundle wagon.

In 1883, he acquired a threshing machine which was powered by an upright steam engine using coal for fuel. To move the machine and engine from one farm to the other, he used two yoke of oxen. Now they had the means to keep the entire family busy to help make a living. Grandpa ran the threshing machine, Grandma ran the sorghum mill and Aunt Nellie supervised the younger boys in stripping the leaves from the cane and topping it. Mother, now 14, did the cooking and housework as well as taking care of the younger children.

Somewhere between 1880 and 1885, she met Reinhardt Keil at some community affair.

By 1885, the Harmison family was able to build a five-room frame house and frame schoolhouses began to replace the first sod ones, which had been built. The United Brethern Church was built in Galatia with a regular minister who came from Hoisington to preach every Sunday. Mother went to Russell to take teacher's training but decided that teaching school was not for her.

She and William Butler were married and they started farming five miles northwest of Galatia without too much success. Water had to be hauled by barrel from three miles away, and with only two horses for power it was an uphill job. Ira, Channie and Florence were all born here. On October 19, 1893, Papa and Ira both were taken ill with typhoid fever. Ira recovered in about two weeks, but Papa was very ill for at least two months. He was delirious most of the time and there were times when Mother had to call in help just to hold him in bed. If one can visualize what Mother must have gone through at this time, with three children under four years of age and water to be hauled. It certainly was a test of the faith and courage she had.

Papa never fully recovered from this illness and in the spring of 1894, as he had not sufficiently regained his strength to do his farm work, he was given the job of township assessor. So the family was able to live without accepting charity.

In 1895, they moved to Great Bend where Papa took a job in the Walnut Creek flour mill. He worked 12 hours a day and received $1.25 per day. They rented at first but later bought a house. During the seven years he stayed on this job, the family increased to six children, and on $1.25 a day they were still able to feed and clothe the family and buy a house. Mother said they could buy calico print material which was used for the girls' and Mothers' dresses, also for the boys' and Papa's shirts for $.02 per yard. A real good pair of shoes could be purchased for less than a dollar and a fair sized sack of corn meal or flour for $.25; subsequently the flour and meal sacks were of course used to make underwear for all of us. Mother knitted our mittens and stockings for winter and during the summer we did not wear stockings. We also did not wear shoes in the summer.

By 1902, Papa's health had failed so badly and the dust in the mill was causing him so much trouble that the doctor ordered him to find something to do that would keep him out in the fresh air as much as possible.

There were still homesteads in Oklahoma Territory, so they sold the house and two lots for enough money to buy a team and wagon. The six kids were loaded along with a water barrel on one side, a crate of chickens on the other side and the family cow tied on behind. We headed for the Territory, as it was called then, where Papa had already filed on 160 acres. I do not know how long it took us to get there but one incident on the trip stands out in my memory and it must be told. It was just before Easter, a freak snowstorm had come on, and we had stopped at a farmhouse waiting for the weather to clear. Evidently, it had been a hard winter and

Traveling salesman.

their livestock had come through the winter in poor shape. This late unseasonable storm had subsequently killed some of their cattle. Regardless of what their own circumstances were, they welcomed us in; kids and all. The farmer's wife and Mother boiled and colored eggs for their children and us. On Easter morning, we had a grand Easter egg hunt.

We arrived in Oklahoma in late April and immediately the neighbors came in to help and sod was broken, a one-room house quickly laid up, and we were at home again. Papa put up fence, plowed ground and planted a crop but to no avail.

The ranchers who were trying to keep the homesteaders from taking up all their pastureland would cut the fences and deliberately drive the cattle into the crop. As I remember, the first year we were able to save our garden. Papa went north into Kansas where it was more thickly settled and got work on a threshing machine.

Hattie, Reinhardt, and Alice

By the next year, the settlers had come in so fast that we were no longer bothered by the range cattle and were able to raise some crop. It was necessary that crops be grown and cultivated with two horses as that was all we had. I think our crop was about two bales of cotton and some corn for horses and cow feed for winter.

Papa's health grew steadily worse and to provide food for the family, as there were now seven children, Mother started doing the washing and ironing for the people who ran the local store which was just about the only work available for a woman. The washings had to be done on the washboard, of course, and the water heated with cow chips, which was the only fuel we had. We kids would fasten a short length of rope to a tub and when the tub was full, we would dump the chips into a pile. The ones who were able to handle the horses would come along with the team and wagon and pick up the piles. The situation grew worse as time went by; food was pretty scarce at times, but we did survive.

In the fall of 1905, Mother knew Papa had to have medical help at once, but there was no money. A kind neighbor lady took Gertrude to hold her baby and drove all day long asking all the neighbors to give what they could to help pay train fare back to Great Bend. With the three youngest children and Papa on a bed in the back of a spring wagon and a neighbor along to take the team back, we started for the nearest railroad station, which was about forty miles away. The conductor and other men on the train helped Mother fix an improvised bed on the train for Papa. We arrived in Great Bend on October 23rd and Papa died the 31st at Grandma Harmison's home.

The first job after Papa died was to get the rest of the family to Great Bend so Mother went back, disposed of what property she could and came back to Great Bend. She went back to Oklahoma several months later to prove up on the homestead.

There was $1,000.00 insurance from the Woodmen Lodge and out of that, she paid burial expenses, bought a modest grave stone and used what was left to buy lumber for a house. Uncle Will and Elmer built the house for just what it cost them to live.

Mother's health had been poor for some time due to very heavy work. She still had seven children to feed and doing the washing and ironing was about the only thing she could do, so she did that until her health broke completely and she had to submit to an operation. Meanwhile, Ira and Channie quit school and got what jobs they could to help. We also raised vegetables and we who were big enough carried them around town and sold what we could of them.

After the operation, Mother, in desperation, bought a second-hand carpet loom and tried to weave carpets. Again we who were old enough helped as we could with threading the loom, winding, and rewinding the carpet rags into balls and winding the shuttles and helping in any other way we could. During this time, we went through whooping cough and Gertrude had typhoid fever.

Mother was constantly under pressure to let other people take some of us kids, especially Mae, as she was the doll of the family. However, Mother was determined to keep us all together, come what may.

The carpet weaving also proved to be too much, and in the fall of 1907, she again went to the hospital for another operation, and this time she was told that her days of hard work were really over. She refused to give up or to allow the family to be separated.

She was recuperating from this operation and wondering where to turn when she received a letter from Reinhardt Keil, the young man she had known way back in her teens. He was a widower with children who needed a mother's care. He had heard that she was alone with children to support, and had written to ask permission to come see her.

What they talked about was none of our business, but they got married at Grandma Harmison's place on February 3, 1908.

We kids were really excited about it; to us he was almost a God. He lived on a

Reinhardt Keil and Hattie Harmison Butler Keil

farm where there were cows, which gave milk to drink, and to make butter and cottage cheese; there were chickens and eggs to eat; to say nothing of hams and bacon and plenty of flour for bread; and best of all, the only thing Mother would have to do was cook for us. There was no more taking in washing, no more carpet weaving, and no more peddling vegetables in town. To us it seemed like a fairy tale, too good to be true, but it was all true.

We moved to Rozell, Kansas where Dad Keil was farming. Almost at once, we began to get acquainted with our new brothers and sisters. The youngest ones at home then were Leslie and Laura; George was living with his mother's sister at the time. They could not speak English and we must have given them a bad time.

As Mother was telling me this phase of her story, she said that when she and Dad were married it was as if a great load was lifted from her shoulders. She knew instinctively that no matter what might happen to her from then on, her children would never go hungry again, and they would always be provided for.

For Mother as well as for us kids it was a beginning of a new life. For the first time in years, she was able to sit down and eat a hearty meal without being afraid that there would not be enough for the rest of us.

There was friction, some jealousy but these two people with patience and understanding made us into a family, and we soon learned there was enough love for all. Not one of us can say that Dad favored his own children over us, and not one of his children can say Mother favored us over them.

In the spring of 1909, we moved to Russell County and for Mother and Dad it must have been like a grand homecoming because we moved back to within a few miles of where they had both first lived when they came to Kansas and where they had first met so many years ago. Dad's friends among the German settlers felt sorry for him, saying that this English woman he had married would break him. These people came to criticize and left singing her praises. They marveled at how, with so many of us to feed and to sew for, there was always good food for as many guests as cared to come or stay to eat. There was not much money for clothes, but we always were neatly dressed and clean.

It was about 1911 when Mother suffered an injury to her left leg, which was to deal her untold pain and misery for many years, sometimes confining her to a chair for weeks at a time.

Seeding in Kansas.

Our home soon became a recreation center for the community. Dad was a wonderful violinist and his favorite songs were the old German folk tunes. The older boys were also musically inclined; they played violin, auto harp and the dulcimer. Almost every evening there was music and dancing, Mother always provided plenty of food, and the young people naturally gravitated to our place. Dad and the boys played for dances and for weddings far and wide. I think that for Mother as well as for us kids, these were the happiest years we had ever known. Her one aim in life had always been to do all in her power for those she loved and her love knew no bounds.

In the spring of 1916 with Henry and Jake in Montana and Gus in Iowa, Dad grew restless and decided to leave. We sold the place and moved to Elkhart, Kansas where Dad saw great possibilities in the fairly new land. But he could not be so happy away from his sons, so that place too was sold and the family moved to Pondera County in Montana, where once again the family was almost all together.

Of the years that followed, I cannot tell very much because Mother did not have much to tell. This I know, that due to extreme drought, times got steadily worse. Finally Mother and Dad with Alice's help, raised vegetables and sold them in stores and from house to house in Shelby. With this money, they would lay in a supply of food for the winter months. Then, as in years before, Mother always

Jake on the dulicmer, Gus on the violin, and Pops (Henry) also on violin at a family reunion in Ledger. They played for many years.

managed to set a table filled with good food for whomever came to eat.

After Dad Keil's death, Hattie spent several years with Alice. Later she went to Arizona and traveled from one place to another whenever she could. During those years, she was always ready and willing to do anything she could to help us. She pieced many quilts, made baby things for many grandchildren, but most of all, she crocheted almost 60 beautiful tablecloths, which have been handed down as family heirlooms.

Henry:

Henry farmed in Otis, Kansas and left for Montana in 1915. Henry Keil, who was known as "Pops" moved his family to Conrad, as he was told there was an individual wanting to sell his homestead rights north of Fowler. This is called a relinquishment. The purchaser of the relinquishment had to finish proving up the homestead rights. Pops bought this relinquishment for $10 an acre from Gene Woodward. The family moved into a home built of railroad ties on the homestead and began farming with horses. The Keil brothers later built a house on what is now called the East Place.

Henry would not allow cards in the house. This goes back to a time when Henry had seen a brother-in-law loose his wages gambling. That family had to do without until the next paycheck. This incident happened in Fowler when the railroad cut was being constructed. Henry came home and destroyed all of his cards. That must have been quite a wager to put such a scare in him.

In 1917, Reinhardt Keil, Henry's dad, and his family moved to Montana and bought a relinquishment from Mr. Kirkpatrick. In about 1928, they moved west to irrigated land and Reinhardt's homestead was taken by the bank. John and

August Keil took over the Reinhardt Keil loan in lieu of a $1,500 deposit they had with the bank at the time the bank went broke. Subsequently, LaVern bought Reinhardt's original place from John and August Keil.

In time, Jake, John and Leslie Keil all homesteaded nearby. Ed Moore, who married Amelia Keil, and August Keil moved nearby, as did Fred Heinitz, who married Gertrude Butler, a stepsister of the Keil's. Lavern and I in time purchased the Jake, John, Leslie and Henry Keil homesteads, as well as Ed Moore's homestead.

LaVern's parents, Henry and Florence were stepbrother and stepsister. Henry's mother, Mollie, died leaving Reinhardt Keil with Gus, Jake, Henry, John, George, Leslie, Hannah, Elma, Amelia and Laura. Florence's father died leaving Hattie Butler with Chauncy, Ira, Louis, Florence, Gertrude, Clara and Mae. These two widowed parents married, blending these families. After they married, they had two additional children, Alice and Ida Keil.

LaVern's fun loving Uncle George Keil died in his 20s from pneumonia. He had been working in the Pondera Valley oil fields.

LaVern, Florence (Moms), Leviene, Calie, and Pops (Henry)

Louis Butler lived in Kansas and died at the age of 15. He was kicked in the head by a horse when he was about 5; he was never right after that.

Henry's brother, Jake had traveled to and been in the Conrad area for a year before sending word to the family in Kansas that land was available. Lavern, then 4 years old, and Henry, "Pops" traveled to Montana in an immigrant railroad car accompanying the livestock, machinery and household goods. Florence, "Moms", and baby Leviene followed on a passenger train.

Immigrant cars were furnished by the railroad to help settle the west. By doing this, the railroads would in turn benefit by creating a need for a way to transport farm and ranch commodities to market, and supplies back out to the settlers. You could load up your household goods, farm machinery, horses, cows or what have you. A person had to ride along with the livestock to care for it.

East Place harvest. Moms standing, Aunt Mae in wagon, and LaVern on wheel. The wagon is backed up to the threshing machine - threshing time.

Jake had become acquainted with and worked for the Gudger family near Conrad. They extended their hospitality to the newly arriving Keil family.

When arriving in Conrad, the immigrant cars were unloaded and articles taken to the Gudger place. While unloading, the chickens escaped. Folks helped catch them as they flew into the window wells of the Herschberg store and a couple other store fronts.

Some of the reasons for taking the land north of Fowler was because it was a downhill trip to haul grain to the elevator. Also, the land appeared to be sandy and would be good to raise corn like in Kansas. Little did they know that in Montana this sand would blow and drift when it was intensely farmed. Eventually huge drifts of sand were on all the fencerows. Because Moms had such breathing problems when the dust filled the house, they moved to Missoula and sold their interests in the farmland to Lavern. Later Moms and Pops lived in Yuma, Arizona during the winters. They were avid rock hounds.

This problem with the sandy soil blowing continued until strip farming was practiced and the use of noble blades began. This equipment became the salvage of the land. In the 1940s, the sandiest land was seeded into crested wheat grass, the cattle herd increased, and reservoirs were built to provide water for the livestock.

There was a good water well at the East Place and the springs that came out of the sandy land toward the Marias River were good. The Dry Fork Creek water was also good year round stock water. At that time, homesteads had man made cisterns to store water for household use, and many places still use these cisterns. At first, the cisterns were filled using horse drawn water tanks. The well at the East Place still holds water. We built a large concrete cistern and were able to have a 32-volt water pump supply water to the house.

Moms loved animals. Their house at the East Place had a sunny front built-in porch. It was fun to see what the guys had brought in after disturbing nests or such by farming. Baby cottontails, baby ducks or pheasants, horned toad, and once a baby curlew; she always had something.

Henry and FLorence's home at the East Place.

Horned toads were often found around the East Place. The kids loved to pet then turn them loose. If you turned them on their back and tickled their tummy, they would become hypnotized.

The curlews were plentiful and fascinating. The cry they made is so wondrous. If you came near their baby, they would fly down to the ground, drag their wing, and try to lead you away from the young ones. They are a large bird and would glide in the air. They are much loved.

Moms was also very proud of being able to trace her lineage to a passenger on the Mayflower. She was a descendant of George Soule, probably a teacher. She went to many of the descendants of the Mayflower meetings in Montana.

LaVern:

LaVern Keil was born in Otis, Kansas, on November 11, 1911 to Florence and Henry Keil. Florence and Henry were known as Moms and Pops as they did not want to be called Grandma and Grandpa after grand kids arrived. Moms had

Transportation of all sorts was used. Moms had the goat and cart; the goat was also milked.

a midwife, Mrs. Bushel in attendance.

In 1915, the family moved to Conad, Montana.

Lavern had two younger sisters, Leviene and Calie. A brother, Tyron, died in infancy. LaVern always regretted not having a brother when he was growing up.

Baby brother, Tyrone is buried near the East place on the fence line to the south.

Moms and Pops went to Conrad one winter to work at the hospital as cook and janitor respectively. They were furnished a bedroom in the hospital; children were not allowed to stay there. At Christmas, the kids, LaVern, Leviene, and Calie, who were staying with Grandma and Grandpa Keil, were allowed to come if they were quiet. LaVern had gotten a sled with a horn for Christmas. It was under the bed. Knowing he should not; he crawled under and honked the horn. The nurse promptly came in and told him to be quiet. This must have made a big impression on him as he remembered it all his life.

When LaVern, Ida and Leviene were staying at Grandma and Grandpa Keil's, Grandpa Keil and Alice went for a walk towards Fowler. Alice had been in the barn with the horses. LaVern, Leviene and Ida stood by the window upstairs watching as they left. Someone, somehow proceeded to roll up tobacco in newspaper to make cigarettes and lit them. The curtains caught on fire. LaVern carried the 5-gallon slop bucket full of potato peelings upstairs to put on the fire. He rushed down and got a bucket of water from the stove reservoir, the drinking water, and all other water and was able to put the fire out. Where did that tobacco come from? Well Grandma Keil smoked Katar tobacco in a little pipe for her sickness. It made her sinus clean out. When Moms and Pops stopped and picked them up to take them home, they were scared of a spanking but did not get one.

LaVern and Leviene earned money by milking the cows and selling the cream. Moms and Pops left home one time--probably for about a week. To earn some money, Leviene baked bread, cookies and doughnuts and sold them and the home brew and almost sold a pig. The buyers came from Fowler. Many were railroad workers, as the work trains would park at Fowler. Leviene earned enough to buy a wooden clarinet to play in the high school band. She paid $30.

Calie and Leviene once decided to camp in a tent in the trees behind the house at the home place. A big lighting and thunderstorm hit and they were mighty scared. They had two dogs at the time-Big Man and Little Man. They went under and into the tent, the big one on top, and they set to howling. The girls were plenty scared too.

George Soule.

There was a shed with a straw roof on it at the East Place. The manure was shoveled out of the shed door and over the hill, as it was built right on the top slope of the hill. Railroad ties were used to build the back of the shed. The sides were boarded up and the rafters were poles with woven wire on top and straw put on top of the wire. It did not have to have roofing and the shed moisture could rise through the roof. It was warm. There was always a big pile of manure just south of the shed, which would have made a great landing spot. LaVern and Leviene got up on the roof, tried to fly with an umbrella off the roof of the straw shed and landed on the manure pile. This did not work too well.

Henry Keil with the binder.

Moms would make capons out of the roosters. Pops did not help-nor did he help with the butchering. He did not like the sight of blood. Moms killed and sold chickens before the Dempsey-Gibbons fight in Shelby and while the arena was being built. She and other farmers sold eggs, bread, butter, milk, and anything else they had extra. She would stop by Grandma Keil's and gather up what she had to sell as well. They had to leave the heads on the chickens so the people would know they were healthy.

Jake and John Keil had gone to Shelby to work on the Dempsy-Gibbons fight arena. On the way home, they tipped over the Model T with a folding top. They were not hurt, tipped the car back up and went home.

The older Uncles, Jake, Gus, and Leslie camped on Moms and Pops place in 1916 and 1917. They were mean to LaVern, as older boys could be.

Why LaVern never smoked! When LaVern was just a little tyke of about seven years old, he learned all he wanted to know about tobacco. As was usual, the Keil brothers hung around Moms and Pops' house. One day Jake Keil stuffed chewing leaf tobacco into LaVern's mouth and made him chew it. He probably cried and tried to get away as Moms discovered the goings on. She ordered Jake to never come around again and always had a grudge against him. This was the end of tobacco for LaVern.

Why did LaVern never drink coffee? Moms often went out of the house to help Pops with the farming. She drove the team of horses many days preparing the soil to plant the crop. Not having hay, the horses were always turned out at night to graze. One of LaVern's jobs was to bring the teams in each morning. When the first tractors came in to the area, Moms urged Pops to buy a tractor and he did. They plowed and used the one-way on the stubble fields, then the duck foot plow for weeding. Pops did the blacksmith work sharpening the shovels on the equipment.

When Moms was out in the field, this left LaVern and Leviene in the house alone and many mornings they made coffee and had a coffee party--lots of cream and sugar. Well, it rained, Moms makes the coffee, and the family sets up to the breakfast table. When asked what he wanted to drink LaVern says, "I'll have some coffee." Now this coffee that Moms made was always good and strong. Moms filled LaVern's cup. "Pass the cream and sugar," he said. Moms said, "You drink it black just like we do." He did drink it black, did not like it and never drank it again.

In 1926, LaVern went to high school in Conrad and stayed with Mrs. Craig.

He helped the janitor at the school, Mr. O'Brien, and earned enough money to buy him a bike and put some in savings. He sometimes pumped the organ for Mrs. Craig at the Presbyterian Church and began attending that church. Later this was to become our church.

For high school the kids from Fowler could catch the train and for $.27 could ride to Conrad, stay in town during the week and if possible, be back home for the weekend by train. Some of them rented an apartment or a little shack and cooked for themselves. They took bread, milk, butter, and whatever they could from the ranch when they went into town. Some of the girls worked for board and room at homes.

About 1929, LaVern got his first car. Moms and Pops took the family to Kansas to visit relatives and friends. On the road home, they ran into real bad weather and muddy roads along the northern Montana route. Some of these roads did not even have gravel on them. Because of these bad conditions, they had to stay over a night. They went shopping and LaVern bought his first car, a Chevrolet roadster, a sort of coupe. The back end opened up and you had a rumble seat. Was LaVern ever popular with his new rig when he got home with it. The girls really liked it. This was the car LaVern and Albert Hedke drove to Kansas with and chased the girls there.

Some of the kids in high school who were LaVern's neighbors were Iverson, Halverson, Nierenberg, and Whitmore.

Lavern's high school picture.

LaVern's high school graduation picture.

Lavern's first car. He bought it in Oswago, Montana coming home from a trip to Kansas when they got snowed in. It was very popular.

East Place house after the porch and kitchen had been built on. LaVern's Roadster on the right.

The Keil boys: Jake, Henry, John, Edgar in front, Leroy, August, and LaVern.

IDAHO GENEALOGICAL SOCIETY
BOISE, IDAHO

HUSBAND

Husband's full name ___ Adam Keil

Born _____ Where _____ Russia

Married _____ Where _____

Died _____ 1869 ___ Where _____

Father's name _____

Mother's maiden name _____

CHILDREN	BORN	WHERE	DIED
1. Anna Katherina Keil	11-9-1839	Russia	1-6-1923
2. Johann George Keil	2-15-1842	Krestowoi Bujeriak Russia	
Children from 2nd wife:			
3. Johann Frederick Keil	1-4-1855	Eckheim Holstein, Russia	
4. Johann Conrad Keil	7-12-1863	Eckheim Holstein, Russia	
5. Johann Reinhardt Keil	6-28-1865	Eckheim Holstein, Russia	

LaVern's family lineage.

These 10 people left Eckheim, Russia for North America October 6, 1876.

Marie Catherine Keil, stepson Johann George Keil, his wife Susan Elizabeth and their children Johann George and Catherine Elizabeth

Sons: Johann Frederick Keil, his wife Maria Elizabeth and their son Johann Frederick

Johann Conrad Keil

Johann Reinhardt Keil

FAMILY GROUP

WIFE   K. E. Kahl - First Wife

Wife's maiden name Marie Katherine Heinitz - Second Wife

Born March 4, 1822   Where Werchnaja Kulalinka, Russia

Died   Where

Father's name

Mother's maiden name

Give full family information and source of information on back of sheet.

This sheet prepared by

WHERE	MARRIED	WHERE	WHO MARRIED
Milberger, Kans.			John Frederick Heinitz I
Milberger, Kans.			Susanne Elizabeth Kuxhause
			Marie Elizabeth Wittman
			Mary Steinert
			Mollie Bauer

Chapter 2
Vivian's family history

Vivian family history:

The Venetz's family came to America on the French ship La Bergone from the port of Le Havre in France in 1891. Matt said they arrived in New York City on his eighth birthday. Eventually they located in Pocahontas, Arkansas. On May 4, 1900 they migrated to Montana. They operated the Swiss Dairy located north of Great Falls, Montana for one year, then bought and operated the West Side Dairy in Great Falls. The West Side Dairy was renamed the Swiss Dairy and run for three years then the name changed again to the Burlington Dairy.

Grandpa Venetz (Alexander and Rosella) came with their family from Reid, Switzerland —first to Arkansas—where they tried to make a living. The climate was not what they were used to. Malaria was a problem.

Alexander Venetz, father of Matthew Venetz.

Uncle Gregor, when thinking about Switzerland, said that the women worked as hard as the horses. Dad only remembers the good things about Switzerland because he was eight when they came to the United States. In Switzerland, the family had Brown Swiss cows. They would take the cows up the mountain in the summer. They would milk the cows and make the cheese there as well.

A couple of the older boys came to Great Falls to visit other families who had

Rosalia Venetz, Matthew Venetz's mother; probably 1930s.

Pocahontas, Arkansas; probably 1894 or 1895, after coming to America.
Front row: Idda, Rosalia, Leona, Matthew, Alexander (two small boys,
twins, Andrew, Ed). Middle row: Matilda, Mary (died in Warm Springs),
Gregor, Melanie Back row: Elizabeth, Adolph.

come to Montana from Switzerland; they found work there milking cows-by hand.
This was a much healthier place, so the family, Alexander, Rosalia and children,
Gregor, Adolph, Matthew, Elizabeth, Mary, Leona, the twins, Ed and Andrew, Idda,
Matilda and Melanie moved from Arkansas to Great Falls.

Alexander bought a dairy along the Missouri River west of Great Falls. On
this place there was an artesian well, so they had a very good cooling system for the
milk. Milk and cream were delivered by milk wagon to their customers in Great
Falls. At first, they dipped the milk out of cans into the customers' containers, as
they drove the milk route. Then milk bottles came into being. It was a real chore
for the girls to wash up all those milk bottles every day. Matt Venetz delivered
milk in Great Falls with horse and wagon. He was able to speak phrases of several
languages, and that pleased his customers. He was proud that the Venetz dairy did
not water their milk down like some others did.

The milk cows grazed all over west of Great Falls and up toward the smelter.
Uncle Gregor's cows grazed the area where the country club is now.

Gregor Venetz married Mary Blank who had come out to Great Falls from Minnesota upon seeing an ad in the Minneapolis paper for maids to work for ladies in Great Falls.

Mary's mother had died when she was 14 and of course, she was tired of raising and caring for the younger children. Amelia Blank (my Mother) came to Great Falls to visit her sister Mary and met (Dad), Matthew Venetz. In 1909, they married and Dad began to run the Burlington Dairy for his mother Rosella.

Dad had traveled throughout Utah and California as a young man. He told of being in San Francisco and helped lay brick for the Palace Hotel. He also told of being in the Salt Lake area. While Matt was traveling, Alexander was herding the milk cows in the area of the smelter in Great Falls. When Alexander got home he was tired and hot, drank some cold artesian well water, and died of a heart attack. Matt came home in 1909

Matthew Venetz and Emelie Blank married in Minnesota on Sept. 29, 1909. Also pictured are groomsman and bridesmaid, Nick and Millie Hinzten.

to help Rosella and his two younger brothers. Ed and Andrew ran the Burlington Dairy. Matt helped run the dairy from 1909-1915.

By 1915, Matt was becoming tired of the dairy. He went looking for his own property. While in Choteau, he heard about the Healey Springs Ranch being for sale. He liked the fact that it had good water, many good springs, and ample grazing land.. Matt and Amelia bought the Healey Springs Ranch and moved their family there. Ed Venetz took over the dairy. The lower part of the ranch was at one time a part of the Flying U Ranch, whose address was Choteau. Zane Gray wrote about the Flying U Ranch in one of his novels. As time went on, they bought other homesteads and enlarged the farm.

The ranch, being on the east end of Porter Bench, was 8 miles southwest of Conrad and had many good springs and lots of available water.

Home on the Venetz ranch, 1940.

Grampy (Matthew) Venetz drank a lot of coffee. The pot was always brewing on the back of the stove. He never washed the coffee pot because he said, "It spoils the next couple batches." They just poured the grounds out, rinsed the pot a little and started a new batch. He used lots of sugar; there was always some left in the bottom of his cup.

First there were granite coffee pots then aluminum percolator pots were used. They used regular grind coffee. Drip coffee pots needed drip grind; a finer grind of coffee.

My mother once told of winning a dance contest when she was sixteen years old. She would have been living in Minnesota then. My girls thought that over, realizing their grandma had been a young girl long ago.

Aunt Mary said my mom was spoiled, as she was able to go to school. Mary was older and had to stay home to care for the younger children. Their mother had died young.

Vivian:

I, Vivian Venetz was born at the Venetz ranch southwest of Conrad, Montana, May 15, 1916 to Amelia and Matt Venetz.

I had an older brother Vernon and a younger sister Florence.

I joined my brother, Vernon, who was five years old. Mrs. Mullins, a neighbor and midwife, came over and was with Mother.

Of course, farming was all horse drawn machinery and there were the range cows. Our first house became a grainery after Dad got the new house built. Thinking ahead, they built the bathroom in the house. We had to carry water in from the well to flush the toilet. But we usually just used the chamber pot, and carried it out. We bathed in the bathtub, heating water in a boiler on the cook stove, and carrying it in to the tub.

Amelia, my mother, was a wonderful loving homemaker. She always had a big garden with vegetables and flowers in it. She always had beautiful houseplants in the bay window. When the hay and harvest crews came, she cooked and baked for the entire crew as well as the family.

One winter, somehow the flour was not loaded on the sleigh at the grocery store when Dad picked up the order in Conrad. The next day, the storekeeper sent it out with Mr.

Vivian Venetz Keil, 1917.

Snortland, a neighbor. His son delivered it on over to our ranch horseback. Was Mother ever disgusted to discover horsehair and sweat in the flour.

Healy Springs School near the Venetz Ranch. Vivian's grade school picture: Mable Snortland, Edith Snortland, Vivian, and Clara Kropp.

Matt was an astute businessman. He ranched successfully. He was an original stockholder of the Farmers State Bank in Conrad.

Our first tractor was a Rumley, called a sidewinder, because the flywheel crank was on the side, not on the front end like most other tractors.

We kids used to tame baby gophers and they ran in and out from under the granary. We would call, "Gopher, gopher," and they would come out.

I was kind of Dad's pet and followed him everywhere, riding

Florence, Vivian, Vernon, 1926 or 1927.

behind him on the saddle horse and on the machinery. I remember how sore my butt was after riding in back of the saddle. I loved to be outside but I also learned to sew, cook, can and embroider from my Mother. One day while on the plow, I was counting the notches on the lever gear when Dad raised or lowered the plow and nearly cut the end off my finger. Dr. Dubois sewed it back on. I can still remember the horses standing there nearly all day, hooked to the plow waiting for Dad to get back.

While at home, one of my chores was riding and tending the cattle. When bringing in the milk cows, one of the horses I rode would run away and sometimes these milk cows came in on the dead run. Sometimes, Dad hardly got any milk that night. I did get into trouble when one of the cows started to give bloody milk. Dad slowed me down. If a fence got in that horse's way he just jumped over it; never dumped me though.

I always liked to get a cup of fresh warm milk right from the cow. Dad would squirt milk at the cats and they could catch it mid-air.

There were wild horse herds out on our range-this is about 1928. They drank water from the sloughs all the time and wondered back and forth towards Krops', but in the summer when the sloughs went dry, the horses came to water at our Healy Springs. We caught several of them and broke them to work. I did some of this when I was 12 or 13, hooking the new horse between two well broke horses on the mower. It made a 3-horse team. The mower was a good tool to use for this. I mowed acres of wild grass hay with a three-horse team.

The hired men used to tease me; probably because I was a brat. One day they put cactus under my mower seat pad. We used old horse collar pads for seat pads. Once they switched the harness on the horses, putting the left hand horse in the right hand position. I was too small to change them back. In retaliation, I not only got even, but made my Dad's day. Dad was sharpening sickle sections on the grindstone. He sat there pedaling the grindstone and I was dripping water on the stone for Dad. The hired men were teasing me with water. I ran to the chicken house which was nearby and up into the loft where the setting hens had hatched out their chicks. Mother had taken the hen and hatched chicks down to the yard. I grabbed some rotten eggs that had not hatched and from the window, took aim, and hit each hired man with eggs. To say the least, they headed for the water trough and Dad just sat there very pleased.

One day our hired man corralled one of the wild horses and broke that horse to ride. I named him Tony and he became my horse. He came with me when LaVern and I got married. LaVern always said Dad gave the horse along with me. Loretta and Charlotte learned to ride on him. All the kids could climb all over him and if they fell off, he just stood. However, Tony hated men and was a different horse when they tried to ride him. He was a really tall horse, so of course the kids always had to have a crawl-on place. One time Loretta was missing, and when I found her, she was hugging Tony's hind leg. He did not move a muscle.

We all went to the Healy Spring School, which ran until 1932. The teacher boarded at our house and we drove old Tip in the buggy to school 1½ miles. Some of the kids were the Snortlands, Krops, Mullins, Barkers, and Gyserts. One year, my 6th grade, there was no school so I stayed at Uncle Gregor's at Ulm and went to school there.

I grew up helping outside on the Venetz ranch so it was easy for me to step up and work along with LaVern farming. Especially during World War II, I worked in the field. The cattle work included feeding, herding, calving. We spent many hours horseback herding, moving bulls and just checking water, pasture and health of the cattle and fencing.

Our community activities were during the winter when we had card parties followed by mid-night lunch and dancing afterwards. We would roll up the living room rugs and go to it. The music was by the neighbors— Tallifsons, Nelsons, Hansons, and Moharts.

The kids would start dancing by standing on Dads feet.

Later on, when I was a teenager, Vernon (my brother) took me to the dances at Bynum, Agawam, Pendroy, and Dry Fork.

Vivian in her high school band uniform. She played a flute.

Vivian's high school graduation picture.

About 1930 Frank Stuart, who ran the grocery store in Ledger, built a big dance hall. After meeting LaVern we mostly went to Ledger.

In 1929, I went to high school in Conrad. I worked for my board and room and $15 a month at Mrs. Berklands for two years. Then the country school closed for good, Florence and I stayed in an apartment at Wieringa's and batched, going home on weekends when possible.

In the country school, I remember having only two pair of socks, one to wear, one to wash. They were long, black stockings and we wore high-topped shoes. Slippers were only for going to town. Montgomery Ward was the source of most of our clothes. The girls always wore a dress. In the winter, the girls who had to walk a long ways could get permission to wear boys' cover-alls under their dress to school and then take them off during school, otherwise they ran the risk of freezing their legs.

In 1945, Mom and Dad bought property at Rollins on Flathead Lake. Matt loved to fish. At first, there was a little cabin right on the lake that they lived in. They loved to have family come and visit and the family loved to go there. Again, there were flowers, garden, raspberries and fruit trees and lots of fishing.

Dad worked on the big house across the road and they moved into it. One upstairs bedroom faced the little creek that fed into Flathead Lake. We all wanted to sleep there; to be able to hear the water bubbling along all night.

Mother, also known as Grammy, always fixed a big breakfast. It would usually consist of German Sausage, special raspberry juice, and pancakes. Dad, known as Grampy, often smoked fish that he caught. When the Fish and Game would come to milk salmon eggs, they would give the fish away to locals. Dad would smoke a lot of them and boy were they ever good.

Grampy always had a pipe dangling from his mouth, kind of like the one Sherlock Holmes smokes.

Dad would walk down the road to buy milk and eggs, and he would walk to Rollins to get the mail. He loved his tranquil home on the lake.

Summer 1959, Grampy and Grammy at Flathead Lake property.

In the Fall, the Venetz family would make sausage and smoke it for the impending winter. Grammy Venetz's recipe follows:

German Sausage

20 pounds of twice ground pork

10 pounds of twice ground beef

1 heaping teaspoon sage

1 heaping teaspoon mace

½ teaspoon cinnamon

½ teaspoon clove

¾ cup salt

3 tablespoon fresh ground pepper

4 cloves of garlic - boil, mash and add to the mixture

Add mustard seeds to taste (we like lots, so we would use about 3 tablespoons)

Mix all together, grind twice and package for sausage patties in the desired size and wrap in freezer paper. If we wanted to stuff the sausage into casings, we would put a casing filler point on the grinder and fill the casing and tie them off for single meal size. The stuffed sausage casings would be smoked for a couple of days, then wrapped with freezer paper and frozen.

Original Dish Pan Sausage (so named because it was the right amount to mix up in a dish pan.)

30 pounds meat: 1/3 beef, 2/3 pork

3 hands salt

1 hand pepper

3 teaspoons sage

1/4 teaspoon thyme

3 teaspoons mace

sprinkle of cinnamon

small sprinkle of cloves

5 cloves of garlic (to taste)

Grind twice

Emelia Blank Venetz Family Tree

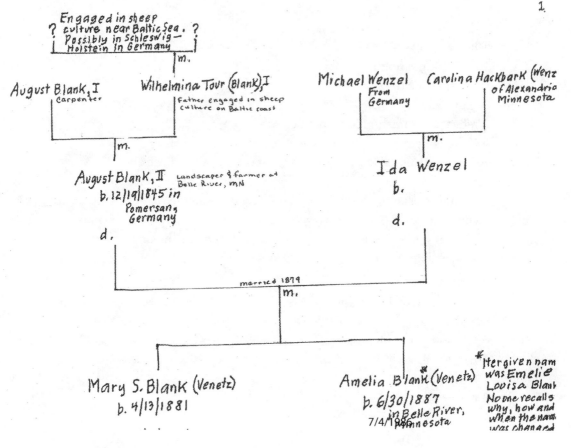

Engaged in sheep culture near Baltic Sea. ? Possibly in Schleswig-Holstein in Germany
m.

August Blank, I
Carpenter

Wilhelmina Tour (Blank), I
Father engaged in sheep culture on Baltic coast

Michael Wenzel
From Germany

Carolina Hackbark (Wenz of Alexandria Minnesota

m.

August Blank, II
Landscaper & farmer at Belle River, MN
b. 12/19/1845 in Pomersan, Germany
d.

Ida Wenzel
b.
d.

married 1879
m.

Mary S. Blank (Venetz)
b. 4/13/1881

Amelia Blank (Venetz)
b. 6/30/1887 in Belle River, Minnesota
7/4/1986

*Her given name was Emelie Lovisa Blank No one recalls why, how and when the name was changed

My Mother's family tree.

Heimatschein
für eine verheiratete Person

Der Burgerrat der Gemeinde Ried-Moerel
Bezirks Östl. Raron, Kantons Wallis, in der Schweiz
urkundet hiermit, daß Vorweiser dieses Heimatscheines Alexander Venetz
Sohn des Clemenz Venetz und der Theresia geb. Imhof
ein Burger dieser Gemeinde ist; folglich als solcher zu jeder Zeit anerkannt und aufgenommen wird;
daß zugleich seine Gattin Rosalia Nelken und ihre Kinder desselben Rechts genießen.
Ausgefertigt zu Ried-Mörel den 29 September 18[illegible]

Signalement:
Alter 54 Jahre
Statur groß
Haare braun
Augen
Nase
Mund
Besondere Kennzeichen:

Der Sekretär: Der Präsident des Rates:

Die Ächtheit obiger Unterschriften bescheint,
Zu Mörel den 4 Oktober 18[illegible]
Der Regierungsstatthalter des Bezirkes:

Der Präsident des Staatsrates des Kantons Wallis erklärt nebst Beurkundung der Ächtheit vorstehender Unterschrift und Siegels, daß obgenannter Venetz Alexander ein Angehöriger des Kantons Wallis ist, und empfiehlt denselben zu guter Aufnahme und Angedeihung obrigkeitlichen Schutzes.

Gegeben zu Sitten, den 5 [illegible] 18[illegible]

Für Der Präsident des Staatsrates abwesend
Der Staatsrath,
J. B. Graven.

Unterschrift des Inhabers:

Alexander & Rosalia Venetz immigration records.

Immigration records for Alexander Venetz children.

(Copy)

— Birth Record —

Taken from the parish record of Morell,
the Children of Alexander Venetz of
Reid Morell and Rosalia Nellen of
Reid Morell, Switzerland.

Venetz, Marie Anna,   born March 24, 1871.
    "   Moritz Gregor   "   December 25, '72.
    "   Adolf Elias   "   December 30, 1874.
    "   Elisa   "   August 8, 1876.
    "   Melania Paulina   "   March 29, 1878.
    "   Maria Elisa   "   February 22, 1880.
    "   Sara Matilda   "   August 2, 1881.
    "   Matheus   "   November 17, 1883.
    "   Theres Louisa (Leona) "   September 17, 1885.
    "   Idda   "   August 24, 1887.
    "   John Edmund   "   December 19, 1889.
    "   Seferin Andres   "   December 17, 1889.

(Lift Switzerland for U.S.A. Nov. 4, 1891.
(Alexander Venetz, born 15 August 1843 – 2 October, 1902.)
(Rosalia Venetz (Nellen) " 8 August 1848)
(Wedding day, 21. May 1870)

VENETZ FAMILY

The following are the children of Alexander and Rosalia Venetz. The information is from a document originating in Switzerland about 1890 when the family migrated to the United States.

Venetz	Melania Ana Maria	Born 20	March	1871
Venetz	Moritz Gregor	25	December	1872
	Adolf Elias	30	December	1874
	Melania Paulina	29	March	1878
	Maria Elisa	22	February	1880
	Sara Matilda	2	August	1881
	Matheus	18	November	1883
	Theres Louisa	17	September	1885
	Idda	24	August	1887
	Johan Edmund	19	December	1889
	Seferin Andres	19	December	1889

Written by Florence Venetz Martin:

I am going to tell you a love story about a handsome young man that was sowing his wild oats in Canada, Utah and California, while a very pretty girl was in Minnesota was being courted by the local butter maker. One day the handsome young man, Matthew, came back to Great Falls, Montana to be with his family as he was ready to settle down. He was greatly surprised when he got off the train to see his brother Gregor meeting a train. Off stepped a very pretty brown haired, blue eyed Amelia from Minnesota to see her sister Mary. Mary was married to Gregor Venetz. Well darn cupid shot an arrow into Matthew's heart. Here was the girl he had been searching for. Matthew got worried when Amelia Blank went back to Belle River, Minnesota as he had a rival in that butter maker. Matthew headed east and rushed the girl of his dreams right off her feet and married her in 1909. Together they ran the Burlington Dairy on the west side of Great Falls, Montana for several years. While there a strapping big son, Vernon was born. They bought the Healy Spring Ranch just south of Conrad, Montana in 1915. Now, an afterthought named Vivian arrived in the story, a brown haired, brown eyed tom boy to join her brother Vernon. Of course, there was a lot of hard work in ranching and farming those days, but Mathew and Amelia still found time for another surprise, a blond haired, blue eyed Florence.

After many years of working and fishing, the three kids married, Vernon to Alice Keil, Vivian to LaVern Keil, and Florence to Willard Martin.

Now Matthew and Amelia decided there must be more to life, so in 1945 they found a place on Flathead Lake at Rollins, Montana where they could fish every day out their back door and raise fruit for the grandchildren to delight in picking. Their many friends and family spent many happy hours at the lake. But the time came when the work there got too hard, so they moved to the Horizon Lodge in Conrad. When the Horizon Lodge opened they were among the first to move in. The Lodge had band entertainment for the residents and guests always visited in the afternoon.

As of this writing, well before 1975, Mathew and Amelia had three children, Vernon, Mrs. LaVern (Vivian) Keil, and Mrs. Willard (Florence) Martin, eleven grandchildren, and 25 great grandchildren.

August and Ida Blank with two eldest children, Paul and Mary; 1881 (Mary was born April 13, 1881).

Blank chilren: Back row: Elizabeth, Mary, Emelie. Front row: Martha, Lena, Paul, Victor.

The Blank boys, cousins of Emilie, would travel from Minnesota to North Dakota to pick potatoes. This was one way young men could earn money. Later my cousins were still going to pick potatoes, girls as well as boys. They would skip school for a couple of weeks.

Matt Venetz as a young man before he ran the dairy.

Matthew Venetz; probably early 1900s, before he married Emilie Blank in 1909.

Emelie Blank before marrying Matt Venetz.

Bell River, Minnesota store. Note the cream cans in the back of the wagons. The Blank family lived near by.

Church located at Bell River, Minnesota. Probably where Matt and Emilie were married.

Matt Venetz on one of the Burlington Dairy milk wagons.

Matt Venetz on the Burlington Dairy milk wagon at Great Fall, Montana.

Buildings were reused by moving them to new homesteads.

Grampy was an avid fisherman. I was born in the house in 1916, and lived here until the big house was built the following year. This house had a bedroom, pantry, with a kitchenette and dining room.

Joe Torgerson threshing machine operation at the Venetz Ranch. He would travel from farm to farm with his threshing equipment and crew.

Torgerson wagon crews at the Venetz harvest.

Torgerson cook house for the threshing crew. We used a cook house similar to this one for our cook/bunk house.

Matt Venetz and daughter Florence.

Me and my horse, Tony before I was married.

Florence, Vernon, Vivian, 1940s.

Vivian, Matt, Vernon, Emelie and Florence Venetz.

Swiss cow wtih bell, 1969.

My cousin, M. A. Duncan at Reider Alp, Switzerland.

Me looking at the Venetz home at Reid, Switzerland built in 1759.

Loretta Keil Grubb and Matt Venetz with his signature pipe share the same birthday, November 18.

Grammy and Grampy holding the day's catch at Rollins.

Grammy at the Rollins home gate at Flathead.

Grampy and Grammy's log cabin at Flathead Lake.

Chapter 3
LaVern meets Vivian

LaVern meets Vivian:

In l934, when LaVern and I were dating, the Grigsby's had met my parents. Dad was a little dark (and he always had a feather in his hat), so they told Moms and Pops to "look out, LaVern's girlfriend's Dad was part Indian." Hearing this, LaVern began to call me his little Prairie Chicken and I called him my old rooster. I'm still his little chicken.

Vernon was so good to take me along to all the dances. In the summer of l933, the 4th of July, I met LaVern at a street dance at the four corners of Conrad. Sometimes LaVern brought Levine and Alice to many of the same dances we came to. That is how Vernon met Alice. Vernon would bring me from the ranch to Ledger, and from the north, LaVern would bring Alice. We continued to do many things together over many years. There were dances at Ledger, Valier, Brady, and in the country schoolhouses. When LaVern was a kid, the Keil brothers, Henry, Gus, and Jake played at dances. They played Dulcimers and violin. They went way out to Dead Indian Coulee to play as well.

LaVern had an Oakland car when we were dating. One day, while necking (1934) in the shade of a building he decided to move the car and low and behold, the back open door hooked a part of the building and "crunch" - well, no more necking. LaVern bent the door back into place and took me home.

LaVern's Oakland, the necking car.

LaVern and I Marry:

On July 1, 1935 a new regulation was in effect. In order to get a

The Marriage Contract

<u>DECLARATION OF MARRIAGE.</u>

We, the undersigned, LaVern Keil whose age is twenty three years and whose residence is Fowler in the County of Pondera, State of Montana, and Vivian Venetz whose age is nineteen years and whose residence is Conrad, Pondera County, Montana desiring to marry each other and to enter into the marriage relation withh/out the solemnization as provided for in Section 5725 of the Revised Codes of the State of Montana of 1921, do hereby declare that our names, ages and residences are as above set forth; that on the 31st day of July, 1935 at Conrad, Pondera County, Montana we the said LaVern Keil and the said Vivian Venetz do hereby agree to marry each other and to enter into the marriage relation, and the undersigned LeVern Keil do hereby take the said Vivian Venetz as my true and lawful wife, and I, the undersigned, Vivian Venetz do hereby take the said LaVern Keil as my true and lawful husband; that no record of the marriage hereby entered into is known to exist and that said marriage has not been solemnized.

LaVern Keil

Vivian Venetz

Witnesses:

Alice Keil

Verna Venetz

Matt Venetz

State of Montana,) SS.
County of Pondera)

On this 31st day of July, A. D. 1935 before me, O. W. Nelson, a Notary Public in and for the State of Montana, personally appeared LeVern Keil and Vivian Venetz known to me to be the persons whose names are subscribed to the foregoing instrumer and acknowledged to me that they executed the same.

IN WITNESS WHEREOF, I have hereunto set my hand and affixed my notarial seal this the day and year in this certificate first above written.

O W Nelson

Notary Public for the State of Montana,
Residing at Conrad, Montana,
My commission expires June 22, 1938.

marriage license a doctor had to guarantee that the couple would never contract a venereal disease. Many couples just hurried up got married before this regulation took effect, or went out of state. Doctors refused to comply; hence, it was impossible to get a marriage license in Montana. There was a choice; you could either leave the state or have a legal contract written up. We chose the contract. This regulation was in effect only three months. Ours was the first contract marriage in Pondera County.

July 31, 1935 we were married at the Venetz ranch, Reverand McCorkle officiated. We went on our honeymoon to Yellowstone Park. On our way, we stopped in Lewistown to visit Leviene. She was in nurses training there. One memory of Lewistown was the pillow fight we had in the hotel, leaving feathers everywhere. We left in a hurry, LaVern driving his Ford coupe. We spent a week there in Yellowstone Park.

LaVern had borrowed $100 to go on the honeymoon trip and we had enough left over to buy groceries. We came home to get ready for harvest. Pops had bought two Baldwin combines-pull type of course, and we cut what crop there was, then went twenty miles east of Conrad to a section of

LaVern & Vivian's wedding picture.,
July 31, 1935.

Wedding day at the Venetz Ranch. From left: Vernon Venetz (Vivian's brother & Best Man), LaVern, Vivian and Alice Keil (LaVern's aunt & Maid of Honor).

state-land Pops had rented there. We took the old cook shack to cook in, a left over from the cookhouse that followed the threshing crews. The Pondera Creek ran by there, so we got our water from there. They farmed this section for 4 or 5 years, hauling the farm machinery back and forth. This is the same land LaVern, Bill Kathman, and Albert Hedke had broke up in 1930-31 using a Case tractor with lugs on the wheels and a disc. They worked day and night to get the harvest done. When that job was done, the guys; LaVern, Bill Kathman, and Albert Hedke, jumped in LaVern's coupe and drove to Kansas to help harvest. On the way down, driving day and night, all at once smoke came boiling up through the floorboards. They flew out of the vehicle to find that a box of matches had got too hot and caught on fire. This was around the 4th of July. When they got to Kansas to help with harvest, they stopped and headquartered at Schlegels, old family friends, traveled on to Aunt Hannah and Uncle Philip Foos's, but it was late at night, so they just laid down on the ground under some trees to sleep,

On honeymoon in Lewistown. We had gone to visit LaViene who was in nurses training at the hospital.

not knowing about chiggers. In the morning, they had many bites and oh how they did itch. They learned to never walk or lay down in tall grass again. Gas was $.25 a

Model A truck, Case lug wheel tractor loaded up to go break sod east of Conrad.

gallon. LaVern drove an old truck that had no doors on it. When it rained harvest came to a halt. They milked cows first thing in the morning, harvested and milked cows again in the evening, and did all sorts of menial chores. Later, of course, they got to take the girls to the movies, plowing through the Kansas mud with chains on to get there.

When it was harvest time in

LaVern breaking sod with the 1934 Model L Case and moldboard plow.

Montana the Schlegle boys decided to head up and help with the Montana harvest.

In 1935 after LaVern and I got married, we moved to the homestead that LaVern owned. He had a couple of milk cows and I had a horse. When we returned from our honeymoon, we moved into our first home which was an old four room homestead shack that LaVern had moved from the Stattler homestead to our homestead. It was on top of a basement that LaVern had dug out and poured cement walls and a foundation. We later put on a porch addition. We moved the barn and corral from Leslie Keil's place to our homestead as well. We also had a building made of railroad ties to house the pigs and chickens.

For water storage, we dug a hole for a cistern, and we just plastered the dirt walls of the hole and we had a hand pump on the porch, which was a big improvement over hauling water in cream cans. This cistern was used for many years until we built a big concrete cistern. By then, we hauled water from reservoirs, irrigation ditches, or Pops' well with a tank on a truck.

The first winter on the homestead was very cold. It remained 20 degrees below zero for most of January. When it finally warmed up many reservoirs were washed out, but none of ours were.

We built on a bedroom, garage, and a bath about 1942. We had to have the bathtub built of stainless steel as we could not buy a regular one because of the war. That tub was so little, tucked inside the bathroom. Everyone loved it.

Rationing during the war curtailed many purchases. Gas was rationed, as well as sugar. You had to have ration stamps to buy many things, or some items were just not available.

In 1935, we bought a Baldwin pull-type combine after the first harvest and had very little money left. Then, in 1936, grasshoppers took the crop. We barely met expenses that year and only had $16.00 left over. LaVern had gone to town and asked the various merchants "I have so much money, can you take a little off the bill?" Some merchants did take a little off the bill and that is how we ended up with that $16.00.

We often walked to Fowler, a couple of miles, for our mail as we had no money for gas or the snow was too deep to drive a vehicle. There were no 4-wheel drives or snowplows; you shoveled your way out of your own trouble many times.

Children:

Loretta was born on November 18, 1936 at the Marias Hotel in Conrad. "I received $100.00 from my father when Loretta was born." This paid the doctor bill and the nurse who took care of us." We rented an apartment at the Marias Hotel in Conrad. I think the hospital was full and we already planned it ahead of time. The nurse wasn't a mid-wife but worked at the hospital and came as a special favor to us, but we paid her. We stayed at the hotel for ten days, as that's how long you stayed in the hospital back then when a baby arrived. We probably got the apartment for $2.00 a day.

Once when LaVern had gone to St Paul to the Farmers Union Elevator meeting, I had put Loretta on Tony, as we had to drive the milk cows to water at the State land reservoir, about a mile away. I ran in to check on Charlotte, asleep, when Tony took off after the cows, got his drink and was on the way home when I caught up, Loretta intact, up on that dear old horse. After that, I took both girls on the horse to water.

"Mrs. Tom Johnson told me she saw Vivian herding horses, horseback, many times while she was very pregnant with me. The Johnson's thought that was why I always loved horses. Years later, the Johnsons gave Charlotte and me our first horse, Janie. We loved her dearly and rode every chance we had." --Loretta

In May of 1938, before Charlotte was born, LaVern was breaking up the land on the homestead west of their present home site. If I turned on the outside light, he was to come to the house and take me to the hospital. On May 24th, I turned on the light and LaVern got me to the hospital in time for Charlotte to be born. Mother had come to stay with Loretta while we were gone.

Donald was born March 4, 1940. We were living at the East Place to feed the cattle.

East Place - Charlotte, Loretta, Don, LaVern & Buck, the family dog.

The snow was deep. LaVern hired Florence Doyle to stay with the girls, and he took me to town. I stayed with Mae and Lawrence Able until it was time to go to the hospital. Donald was born at the St. Mary's hospital in Conrad.

Not being a horse lover like the girls, he ran our jeep and hunted many jackrabbits at night with friends. In high school he would have friends out, they would hunt bobcats and whatever, and then we would cook it at home. Coyote hunting was always on the agenda. We always had our house full of young people. We would have hayrides, skating parties, ping-pong contests; you name it. Donald was great with plans of farming with new seed variety development. We all rogued, pulling out any foreign plant or grain. Once Don and Louie Puzon were pulling foxtail out of the Russian wild rye. So much money a plant, then I discovered they split up the foxtail plants. So much for enterprise.

As told by Don, "I was about seven and Dale about two when Dad confronted me about smoking in the barn and trees. He said 'We cannot have you burn down the barn, so I want you to smoke at the kitchen table. Because you are stealing the hired men's cigarettes, I will buy you some today.' It sounded good to me! I was waiting for him when he returned with a bag of assorted tobacco. As we sat at the table, I lit up a smoke, blew smoke in Dale's face and felt like a king. Then

Dad gave me the payment receipt for like $2.50 or $2.80. Then he said, 'You will have to pay me back for this with your $.25 weekly allowance.' Well, I also liked my candy every week and that was five candy bars worth for two to three months. So we made a deal, I was done smoking and he returned the tobacco, No charge."

Don graduated from Montana State University and he and Kay came home to work on the ranch.

Dale was born January 21, 1945 in the St. Mary's hospital; Dr. Dubois was attending. We were building the crib granary at the time. Glen and Clara Feda were visiting and gave me a bumpy car ride, which they said, would bring on the baby. It seemed to work as Dale was born the next day.

Dale could do limited phases of the

Charlotte, 1 or 2 years old.

Loretta, Vivian, Donald, LaVern, & Charlotte (1943).

farming. Because of his allergies, he was limited to some jobs. He preferred wheels over horses. I remember his little back was sore from hanging over the Jeep seat edge to reach the peddles so he could drive.

Dale went to Law school so he could have a profession other than farming due to his allergies. He graduated in 1969, moved to the ranch, and began his law practice, commuting to Conrad.

He helped with the seeding and harvest while LaVern and I continued managing the ranch.

Mrs. Colville came many summers to help out with the cooking and care of the children, who loved her very much. She crocheted dresses for the girl's dolls. She was a neighbor of Moms and Pops at Orchard Homes in Missoula.

Family stories:

LaVern, Charlotte, Loretta, Vivian, Donald, & Dale. This was the day Florence and Willard Martin were married at our house, 1949.

When I see our beautiful courthouse in Conrad, this memory comes to me. Mr and Mrs. Abraham, who owned the grocery store, invited my family to the Chautauqua which took place on the vacant lot where the courthouse is now. This traveling group put up their tents and performed plays, sang, spoke, and sometimes had a comedian. It was a very special evening of entertainment. It would perhaps be a combination of "Shakespeare in the park" and

Vivian & LaVern.

"The Virginia City Players".

We went again when this group returned. The Webster Collegiate Dictionary describes the Chautauqua as an institution of the late 19th early 20th century event providing popular education in the form of lectures, concerts and plays, often presented outdoors or in a tent.

The story of how LaVern became known as Choppy. This event happened at the Fowler country school. A big wind storm blew and made huge drifts of sand. The kids decided to dig holes for the coyotes to fall into. The children had not chosen the perfect season to accomplish this task, as the ground was frozen. They had to use both a shovel and an axe. Leviene stepped up to see how it was going just as LaVern chopped down with the axe, and it just caught the toe of her shoe. The kids all called him "Choppy" after that. The name followed him throughout his life. Some people did not even know his given name. Even to this day, some old timers call him "Choppy". Friends hardly ever called him LaVern, always "Choppy." When our children went to high school, they were called "Choppy," especially Loretta. Once, one of Dale's girlfriends called and asked for "Choppy" and I had to ask her, "Which one?"

In 1936, we took 100 horses, George Wood's, in on pasture. We used the grass down toward the Dry Fork, and then let them out east of Fowler, as that was kind of free range. We grazed all the grass up to the Levett place, later Tweets, and Iverson's. I herded these horses. We finally got a would-be cowboy to help watch them for a share. They did get into Iverson's field once, then, once they took up the road toward Conrad, so Mr. Woods took them home. Our "cowboy" had ridden off to town for a day or two.

In l936 and 1937, the gypsies would come through our place on their way down to the Marias River, staying at the railroad bridge area. They would stop and visit and we would give them a chicken or two and some milk, wheat and sometimes flour. They would stay a couple weeks, then come back through, visit and see what we had to offer them. If we were not home, a chicken or two would sometimes be missing. These folks came in a covered wagon pulled by a team of horses. There would be several wagons and families.

In l937, we had a short crop and no money, but decided to go to the circus in Conrad. LaVern cut a few bushels of wet wheat and took it to Fowler. Mr. Zimmerman took it, but I bet he shoveled it around for days and we did get to the circus after all, thanks to him.

There were times that we had to do whatever we could to make sure the cattle had enough to eat. We could burn the spines from the cactus during the dry years in the spring, and use them as an alternate feed. Calves loved them and the cows would eat them, as the cactus was sweet and edible after we removed the spines.

When we got the first Model A truck we both noticed that it was a big step up from the horses for doing rock hauling and so on. One day the cows got into the wheat field at Grandpa's place. When LaVern was chasing them with the truck, one old cow stumbled and fell. Well, LaVern ran over her and was stuck, and had to walk home for help to pull the truck off; needless to say, the cow was dead. Ever after, he always warned everybody, "just don't run over one, let alone hit one."

A summer trip to Great Falls would always involve a picnic at the Teton River because it was about half way. We would always stay a week and visit relatives.

Before antifreeze was available, in the winter the radiator of a vehicle had to be drained every time the rig was turned off, to prevent the engine from freezing up. To restart the engine, boiling water had to be added to the radiator. Sometimes boiling water had to be put in two times before the engine would start.

I went out to run the tractor the night shift and brought Donald, then about 2, along. We had refueled, drained off the extra oil, we were burning crude then, and I was about to go when Donald backed into a dead cactus. He got his little butt full of those dead stickers. LaVern and Aunt Gertrude pulled a bunch and finally took him to Dr. DuBois in Conrad. Don would say, "There's another one." All this time I was going around and around the field.

We had a fuel tank mounted on an old vehicle chasis with a ball hitch on the front. We could pull it around with the pickup to the fields to fuel the tractors. This one time, LaVern just dropped the hitch onto the pickup ball to move the fuel tank a short distance to the trail at the end of the field. The hitch jumped off the ball and the trailer rolled down the hill with LaVern running after it. The whole fuel trailer tipped over and began to leak precious fuel out of the vent pipe in the top of the tank. I quickly stuffed rags into the vent pipe trying to save the fuel. The men hustled fast to upright the fuel trailer. They were successful and the work continued. Always double check to make sure your hitch is secure.

We did have an icehouse, made of railroad ties, which we used until we got a propane refrigerator. The neighbors helped in putting up the ice every winter. The ice was covered with sawdust in the icehouse. It would last up to July--so had an icebox to keep milk and cream in.

If the ice was thick enough, it was sawed and hauled from the reservoirs, otherwise from the Marias River. The icehouse was built out of railroad ties. It had been brought up from Fort Conrad.

"The uphill or west end of the ice house had a little room with and outside door. We used it for a little playhouse. It was just right for Loretta and me to play in with our dolls. It had a shelf around the wall and we had a little aluminum cabinet for our play dishes. We also hung blankets around the oldest, wood wind charger for a place to play with our dolls, buggies, etc."--Charlotte and Loretta

Larry Able was working for us cleaning the manure out of the East place

Old Model A truck. The fuel tank was on an old truck or car frame. This is the one LaVern rolled. One combine was Pop's and one was LaVern and Vivians. They worked together for harvest.

barn, hauling the manure out to the fields, and spreading it. Larry recalled filling the manure spreader by shovel when LaVern drove up, grabbed a shovel and started shoveling. All of a sudden he announced "It's a boy! It's a boy!" and that of course was in reference to Don's birth.

The Venetz's would often play tricks on others. Once when we went to Great Falls unbeknownst to us Arnold and Melvina came to visit and we were not at home. They took our pick-up and parked it crossways inside the little stone shop. It took quite a while to get it back out, as there were only a few inches between the

Matt Venetz and Henry Keil

crossways pick-up bumpers and the shop walls.

In retaliation, we found them gone when we went to visit them one time. We piled all of their horse-drawn machinery we could move right in front of their house door; they couldn't get in when they came home.

Arnold and Vernon Venetz wired up their car wheels to the battery of the car, so that when the dogs came to pee on their wheels, the dogs would get a shock.

In the Venetz barn door, there was about a ten-inch hole to reach through so one could unlatch the door. The cats used that hole as their way into the barn. Arnold and Vernon electric wired the hole and poor cats would get a surprise.

When Gregor, Adolph, and Dad were young and living at the Great Falls dairy, they pulled tricks. One Halloween, they took the wheels off the neighbor dairyman's wagon and put his milk wagon up on the roof.

They put water or sugar in fuel tanks, and it would stick up the motor. They would let air out of the tires. If they thought of it, they would figure a way to execute the trick. Their sisters' boyfriends were prime targets.

Harvesting with new tractors, pull combines and pickups. Foreground pickup is a 1938 Ford.

Another story Larry shared with us during our 50th wedding anniversary was about going to a movie in Conrad. During supper, we decided to go to the movie, but first, the men had to shovel off a load of wheat, and the gals had to do the dishes. Boy did the shovels fly. We made it to the movie on time.

I had bought a purple suede coat that LaVern really liked. At Christmas, that year, a white Lincoln car with a purple top was delivered to the ranch. When I looked out, I saw a shiny new car with a great big bow on it. Clayton and Hannah Giskas and family were good friends of ours and would come out hunting pheasants and deer on the ranch. Clayton worked at the dealership in Great Falls and delivered the car. He also delivered the "big bear," which was a giant stuffed bear almost five feet tall. I hid the bear, planning to bring it out at Christmas, but Mark and Terri, Loretta's children, had been playing upstairs. They opened the closet door and saw "big bear." I will never forget the sight of those two little pairs of eyes as they flew down the stairs. They said "Grandma, there is a big bear up there!" We brought "big bear" downstairs and it became a living room fixture for all of the grandkids to snuggle, hold and play with. That bear was the greatest babysitter we ever had.

Loretta's son, Jay enjoyed riding his motorcycle and four wheeler along the breaks while helping herding cattle.

One morning LaVern loaded a tie cross ways on the back of the jeep and left to fence. He returned hours later acting loopy and had a big lump on his head. We tracked him back along the fence and found he had driven too close to the fence and caught the end of the tie, which swung around and hit him in the back of his head.

I believe it was the Minnesota boys who had been at the Little America bar all evening. On the way home, they saw some honeybee hives, they grabbed a box and put it into their car, bees and all. During the trip the bees were upset, were buzzing around, and got in a sting or two. They arrived at our house all proud of their prize. I paid the honeybee man with an apology.

Family Dogs:

Our St Bernard, Chief came from Spokane where he was a little big to fit into the neighbor's flower gardens. The hired men used to slip him snacks from the table. When any salesman came to the yard, he would greet them eye to eye, keeping them right in their car.

Shep was an Australian cow dog. He was worth several horses and riders when it came to flushing cattle out of the brush. He and Chief would gang up on rattlesnakes; each on opposite sides. They would throw it into the air until the snake was dead. As Shep got older and slower, a snake finally bit him.

Cookie was a cute little Pekinese dog. She was the only dog allowed in the house, but only to the edge of the carpet. Poncho was another Pekinese we had at the same time. When he came, we rigged up a heated dog house.

LaVern had a lot of horses through the years. Pinto was a tall tri-colored paint. They were a fine sight heading to the East place or herding cows. He hardly ever walked, just a constant jig.

Beauty was a wonderful and fast cow horse. LaVern used her during calving to bring a cow into the corral. One day he made a fast turn on ice with her and the pair went down. Beauty was fine, but LaVern had broken his ankle. Beauty had a running walk gait also known as single footing, and could cover a lot of ground. She required an experienced rider.

Neil Snoddy & Chief, our St. Bernard. Chief was in trouble in Spokane, so he spent the rest of his life on the Keil Ranch.

I would order baby chicks and raise them into fryers. We would have chicken almost every day. The hired men loved these meals. When the men would get in early, the chicken would still be in the frying pan. Two of those men were brave enough to get a fork and stab the gizzard, as it was a prize piece. I finally had to run them out of the kitchen.

A rainy day was a chicken butchering day. The hired men did not relish this day. Before we had freezers, we would can the chicken in quart jars.

Charlotte, Donna Lee, & Loretta on Janie. LaVern on Pinto.

One April fool's morning, Louie came into lunch after trailing the calves to water. He told the kids that it was so cold that when he whistled a tune on the way to the water, it froze in the air and he heard it on the way back; April Fool's!

Around 1950 LaVern was thinking of trading cars. The entire family went along and we tried out a new car up Gore Hill to the airport from the Lincoln dealership in Great Falls. Then we drove the old car up Gore Hill for comparison.

On the way down the hill with the old car, LaVern attempted to pass a pickup, which turned in front of our car. This forced us off the road, down the embankment, tipping the car; nose first, up onto its roof. We escaped with cuts, bruises, a broken nose, bruised knees etc. Glass was in everything. We were sure a bandaged-up family.

To add insult to injury, we had a case of eggs in the trunk. Some of the eggs did not break, but some adventurous eggs found their way to the front seat of the wrecked car. A nearby lady gathered up the best of the eggs. The eggs were a small "thank you" for helping us. We then had to get the new car.

As told by Loretta, "One summer Dad decided we needed a "real ranch cook." I am not sure what Mom thought, but dad wanted mom available to help him. Well, Dad hired a "real ranch cook" and it was an eye-opener for all of us. She was really upset that we did not have assigned seats at the table. Also, she made pies with scanty filling.

However, Dad did not complain because he had hired a "real ranch cook." The cooking was not like Mom's, but we were all pretty quiet. The best was when Mom and Dad left for the day and the cook made Louie, the hired man, sit in Dad's place at the head of the table as she had become enamored by our dear Louie. We kids thought it was all amazing and could not wait to tell Mom."

Vivian, the "real ranch cook."

One day when I was out checking the irrigation ditches, I noticed a large Northern Pike. I went and got my shovel and whacked that nice big fish in the head and we had a very tasty supper. It had made its way down the ditch from Lake Frances.

We have always enjoyed dancing. One of our favorite bands

LaVern and Vivian Keil Family Tree

Loretta M. Grubb (W. Erling Grubb)

I. Mark E. Grubb (Devra DeVries)
 1. Kristi Ann Grubb (Stephen Calvery)
     Calista A. Calvery
     Alexis Mae Calvery
 2. Garth N. Grubb
 3. Garrett M. Grubb
 4. Grant Grubb
 5. Graham Grubb

II. Terri Kay Grubb (Randy Prewett-divorced)
 1. Whitney J. Prewett
 2. Justin J. Prewett
     (Jeremy Reed-divorced)
 3. Cashlee Redd
 4. Shaunee Redd

III. Jay David Grubb (Cynthia Nickol)
 1. Angela Grubb
 2. Bethany Grubb
 3. Erica Grubb
 4. Jackson Grubb

IV. Ross W. Grubb (Jill Armbruster)
 1. Jessica Grubb (Sergio Moreno)
 2. Emilee R. Grubb
 3. Dylan Grubb

Charlotte L. Marshall (Robert J. Marshall)

I. Clay Marshall (Amy Slaughter)

II. Ward Marshall (Paige Brooks-divorced)
 1. Thomas Marshall
         (Amy Jorns)

III. Gwen Marshall (Bill Morrison)

Henry LaVern Keil and Vivian May Keil

Donald H. Keil (Kay Throcknorton-divorced)

I. Helen Keil (Shawnn Hoye-divorced)
  1. Serena Keil-Hoye

II. Jennifer Keil (Rolland Schlepp)
  1. Cavin Schlepp
  2. Katie Schlepp
  3. Kylie Schlepp

      (Louella Danbrook-divorced)
      (Joselyn Sajulga-divorced)

Dale L. Keil (Sheri Gemar Keil-divorced)

I. Kent Keil (Lisa Huntsinger-divorced)
  1. Amber Keil
  2. Alyssa Keil

II. Brent Keil (Jana)
  1. Katelin Keil

      (Patricia Dean)

was The Happy Four from Choteau. We danced at the Moose Hall in Conrad and Square danced at the Ledger Community Hall.

LaVern at about 90 years old.

When I came down with the shingles I couldn't write, I could barely make out a check. I couldn't sign it. Shingles is the inflammation of the nerve endings, extremely painful. They came out like eruptions, like the small pox. They radiated from the middle of my back, from the spine, all the way across my back to the front and the rib cage. I remember I had a terrible cold sore at Thanksgiving. You can't have shingles unless you had the chicken pox.

LaVern also had the Shingles. We had driven to Missoula with about six cows to go to Mom's and Pop's orchard place. On the way home, LaVern began itching and hurting. We stopped in Conrad and the doctor said it was Shingles.

At that time, many of the people who had gotten the Polio shot developed Shingles afterwards. LaVern was one of these.

Sometimes it would pay to watch a boiling pot. I always tried to make good use of my time. I figured I could put some eggs on to boil, go saddle my horse, the eggs would be done and ready to shut off before I left. They would be cooked, cooled, and ready to make salad for lunch. Well, I forgot the eggs and headed out for the East Place, three miles away. Upon reaching my destination I remembered those eggs.

I kicked that Pinto horse in to a good lope and headed home, fast, but alas the eggs were history. They were blown up and were even on the ceiling. Boy did the house smell bad. There were no cooked eggs and no completed riding projects. Just a mess and a stinky house.

Chapter 4
Fowler

Fowler:

The town of Fowler was named after a pioneer sheep rancher, B. R. Fowler in 1908. In 1910, the Fowler post office was established. The Fowler post office was first in Choteau County, then after redrawing county lines, it fell within the

Fowler Mercantile store & hotel.

Pondera county lines. Oscar Fluto was the first postmaster.

Later postmasters included Mrs. Gordon, Alice Keil in the early 1930's, Munson in the 1940's, and Bill Riggs. The outgoing mail would be hung out for the mail train attendant to catch. The man in the mail car could hook the mailbag from the moving train. He would then throw the incoming mail from the car. The Fowler post office also had a rural mail route going out East. One of the route couriers was Joe Love. Post Master Mrs. Gordon lived on top of the hill South of Fowler. Later the Fowler Post Office closed and the mail was sent to Ledger.

Those on the West side of the Dry Fork that were Fowler customers were added to the North Conrad mail route. Mr. Wierenga was the mail courier on that route for many years. I stayed at his family home in Conrad when I went to high school. Mail was first delivered using a team, especially in the winter, as the roads were not paved or plowed as they are now.

Until Loretta started school in 1942, we spent the winters at the East Place as there were barns for the cattle--about 40 head--and there was water at the Dry Fork. LaVern would ride horseback to Fowler and get the mail and a few groceries. At that time, there was the Post Office, store, elevator and the railroad section house.

When Alice got married to Vernon Venetz, my brother, the Munsons ran the Post Office. When the Munsons quit, Bill and Calie Riggs ran it.

The elevator was operated by Bill Zimmerman.

Some of the people who came to Fowler were; Leslie, Jake, LaVern, and Henry Keil arrived in 1915. Reinhart Keil arrived in 1917. Charley Myers family, Frank and Russel Meyers, Ivo and Francis Norton, Trebbles, and the Kluths, made some of the home brew.

Elevator man, Bill Zimmerman & Henry Keil.

More of the people that came were Fred Flickinger, Hudson, the Watkins man, George Williams, and the Gordons were just up the hill east of Fowler. McCrackens, Flutos, the postmaster who then later ran the store. Halvorson, Neirenbergs, Iversons, Ed Moore, Carl Levetts, Stattlers, and the Zimmermans ran the grain elevator.

The Quinnamans ran the lumberyard. Jarvis, Morrison, Matt Bedner, a trapper, Cassiday, West, Triplets, and the Warens who lived down where the Dry Fork runs into the Marias, B.R. Fowlers, who the town is named after. Hasketts, Tornga, who lived on top of the hill just west of Fowler. The Chicks lived east of Fowler.

Many of the homesteaders who did start the settling of the area were located by Sam Sollid, the area locator. Sam could show the homesteaders where the cornerstones of the 320-acre parcels were located. He would meet them with his wagon, show them what was available and help them with the process of filing and getting started. He had a homestead himself in Flat Coulee. Loretta and Erling now own that parcel of land. Each homesteader usually got 320 acres.

The Fowler store was a popular meeting place with a round pot bellied

Buildings were reused by moving them to new homesteads. Nothing was wasted.

stove for heat. Supplies were delivered by rail and pickles were delivered and sold from a barrel. At one time Cliff Kluth ran the store and had home brew available. Oscar Fluto ran the store, then Bill Riggs, who was the last one to run the store before it closed.

The gas well north of Fowler:

Investors were brought by train to observe. It was a place to go to watch the drilling activity. When the well was drilled, oil was not found, but natural gas was. For many years, you could toss a match down into the hole and get a flare; apparently, the well was not properly plugged. I understood there was enough gas to be used as the power for drilling.

Homesteading:

Farming was done with horses. Not all of the land could be broken up for farming, as some land was not suitable and some had to be reserved for grazing the stock. Winter feed had to be planned for or purchased from the Lake Francis irrigation project farmers. As a result, one could not make a living on 160 or 320 dry land acres. About 1920 many borrowed all of the money they could, and moved on and let the land go. Some was taken

The gas rig was east of East Place across the railroad, southeast of the underpass and ran on natural gas.

Investors arrive to look at the Fowler gas well.

over by the counties for taxes or by land agents. Pops began buying up some of these homesteads, and LaVern continued to do so as the settlers moved on. Moms encouraged Pops to buy a tractor, or they would have to give the land up. That was the turning point for Moms and Pops because they could work more land and have more land in crops.

A homestead was originally 160 acres, however, later changed to 320 acres. The homestead had to be lived on and improved on for five years by the filer before

This binder was pushed by horses in the Conrad area. Leslie Keil on binder, Henry Keil on tractor, LaVern standing, & Albert Hedkey on drills.

ownership was transferred to their name. The increase in acreage was made because the land was not fertile enough to make a living on 160 acres. Pops paid $10.00 an acre to Gene Woodward for his homestead northeast of Fowler, which was the beginning of the Keil Ranch. The family moved into a shack built out of railroad ties on the ranch

northeast of Fowler, began farming with horses. Later, the Keil brothers built a house near where the shack was; now called the East Place.

Many of the nearby homesteaders lost their mortgaged land to the bank and the bank interests were taken over by a mortgage company. The mortgage company rented the land to Pops and he later bought the land - the West Place and the Fowler Place.

In 1929, the year LaVern graduated from high school, Pops bought a model "L" Case, which allowed them to farm a lot of land that had been previously used to graze the workhorses. LaVern had been helping his dad all this time and eventually filed on his own homestead when he turned 21. Pops bought Uncle Leslie Keil's land in 1934, took the first crop, and then let LaVern buy the land for the same amount. He also rented and farmed the Reinhart Keil land.

When the Valier irrigation project was put in, it was decided it would be impractical and too expensive to put water across Flat Coulee. That is how come our place and area was put up for homestead. Most homesteads were 320 acres. However, our home place was so rocky and hilly; we got a section, 640 acres.

This L Case with drills was LaVern's first tractor.

Ice:

Many people had an icehouse; they would cut the big cubes of ice on either the river or a reservoir, and then bury it in sawdust in an icehouse. We had ice until midsummer. We had an icebox and an icehouse made of railroad ties, with a pile of sawdust inside.

It was a great time when neighbors got together for cutting ice and filling their icehouses. The women would cook up a big feast that day.

The railroad at Shelby had a big icehouse and they put up lots of ice from the river. While they filled up with coal (from Canada), water from the water tower, and passengers, they iced up too.

Schools:

There were two Fowler schools. One was north of Fowler on the Henry Keil place, which was later moved out west by Whitmores and August Keils. For a few years, school was held in Fowler. There was also a Fowler school in Toole County, Northeast of Fowler.

Students and families had a little campfire once in the Fowler schoolyard for roasting marshmallows. When Reinhardt Keil got his roasted and tried to eat it, it got all stuck in his beard and whiskers. Leviene thought that was real funny. The Fowler school was about one-half mile west of East Place it was called the Bum Ridge School. The Bum Ridge School got its' name because the first man that

Fowler school located west of the East Place was also known as the "Bum Ridge School."

homesteaded the East place brought bums in to work the land. The bums lived in an old shack. It was hard times and a lot of people around town were out of work.

Skunks got under the Fowler School house once. Dogs got after the skunks so there was a big stink; years later the books still smelled like skunks.

The school was later moved south of the feed lot-on the corner by the County Road. Later the Grigsbys bought it and moved it South a mile and used it for a grain bin.

Loretta and Charlotte first attended the Pioneer School four miles southwest of home, then all four of the kids went to the Fowler School, one and a half miles south of our home.

In 1942, Loretta started school at the Pioneer School, four miles west. Charlotte was next. We no longer stayed winters at the East place, we just rode over horseback or later took the Willy jeep to care for the cattle. Many times when the weather was favorable, bicycles were hauled to school in the morning and the kids peddled home after school in the afternoon. Flat Coulee was about half-way home from school. There was a big curve in the road on the west side of the coulee. There would be big mud ruts in the road after a big rain. Charlotte, then a first grader, lost control after being caught in a rut with her bike. She had a awful wreck, knocking her out cold. This was near the bottom of the hill where a small creek ran. Loretta, a third grader, got her handkerchief wet in the creek and tried to dab some of the blood and dirt away. She then loaded Charlotte on the cross bar of her boys bike and began the task of pushing her load home the last two and one half miles. The wind was blowing hard and luckily a neighbor boy, Bobby Flickinger, came by with his car and gave them a ride home. Charlotte woke up at home a few hours later with extensive road rash on her face and hands. She was always so thankful for her sister's apt help.

Charlotte and Loretta riding Pinto and Patsy.

A schoolhouse was bought and moved to the south of us 1 1/2 miles. This was called the Fowler School. The students came from these families: Frank and Evelyn Myers (Dennis, Sharon and Jim), Russel and Ethel Myers (Jerry, Marion and Hazel), Ivan and Frances Norton (Harold and Robert), LaVern and Vivian Keil (Loretta, Charlotte, Donald and Dale). Dawn DeGrey attended when her mother Jane taught. Clara Metvet was another teacher at the Fowler School. Marilyn Sigety attended the school in 1948 when her Dad helped to construct the brick house.

The schools were an important fixture in the community. They served as gathering places for social functions. Every so often schools would have dances for the young folks. All had lots of fun with school dances held at the country schools with music supplied by local people.

Country schools always had a Christmas program; it was a community highlight. One end of the room was divided off with bed sheets hung on a wire. The teacher chose three or four plays as well as poems and songs. Parts were assigned and the children memorized their lines. What an exciting night! All the neighbors and hired men came and the program was presented. Then Santa would come. The Dads took over the Santa Claus job. LaVern's first Santa experience was at the Fowler school. When giving out gifts, Dennis Myers announced, "Santa has on Choppy's boots".

These were one-room schools with two outdoor toilets, one for girls and one for boys. Country schools were usually taught by one teacher. She had all eight grades. Many schools had a teacherage attached to the back of the school house for the teacher to live in.

The next Christmas program was at the Ledger School. When the Grubb family came in, Jay was just so excited to announce, "We saw Santa's deer just up the road". Aren't kids the most endearing?

LaVern served on the school board of Fowler, district 54, then later on the board of District 10.

Dale had to complete his eighth grade in Conrad as the Fowler school had closed.

High School Days of the 50's and 60's:

We had lots of young people come out to the ranch. They enjoyed the shuffleboard game that was inlayed into the floor, ping-pong and roller-skating in the basement. We had ice-skating along with a hayride, wiener roasts and lots of hot chocolate. We had slumber parties, horseback riding, hunting bobcats, coyotes, gophers and magpies, and hiked in the hills fossil hunting. You name it, they did it. We always welcomed them and had fun, too.

Hardships:

In l937, with the crop so poor, the grasshoppers got a lot of it. We bought a bunch of wiener pigs and put them out on Uncle Leslie's place to graze. The old chicken house was there and some water in the reservoir. They did real well, we had made a good deal. Some folks north of Cut Bank brought in turkeys and herded them out in their fields.

In 1935, LaVern shot jackrabbits-there were lots--skinned and stretched the hide. We sold the hides for $.25 each. The cream and hides bought the groceries for us. We saved enough money to buy a load of crude oil (used in the model L Case tractor) from Gus Blaze's well, northeast of Shelby. Pops loaned the seed to put our first crop in. The first wheat that we sold was for $.34 per bushel. This was the lowest price we ever sold for.

LaVern picked rock with a pick during the evenings, including Sundays, during the early years, but I did my share of picking and hauling rocks, too. In 1938, LaVern broke the one-half section West of the house. Uncle Leslie had only 50 or 60 acres broke out, so they had to pick rocks on all the rest and break it out. The George Williams and Grandma Flickinger's lands were the same with only a small acreage broke out and farmed. LaVern worked months getting that land ready to farm.

Whenever land was purchased, LaVern, myself and our hired help hauled rocks for weeks.

In 1936, May 15, on my birthday, Whitey Louchs from the hardware store came out with a gasoline powered washing machine tied to the bumper of his car—I was no longer scrubbing on the wash board and boiling the clothes in a wash boiler on the stove. "How lucky I was"--Vivian.

Money:

"There wasn't any." - Vivian.

Water:

Water, of course, was short, so we all took a bath in the same water; hey we had a rubber-folding bathtub. Then you could scrub the floor, water the flowers or give it to the pigs. After scrubbing vegetables, the water was always used twice. We got all the use out of the water we could.

When the add-on bathroom was done, of course, we needed a bathtub but could not requisition one—war time. So, we had a stainless steel tub built in Shelby.

By that time we had 32-volt electricity-wind power.

We built cisterns for household use and hauled water from reservoirs, when fresh, the irrigation ditch and, in the winter, from Conrad. You learned to be water thrifty. We had a hand water pump in the porch that pumped water up from the cistern into the house. When we built the new cement cistern we installed a 32-volt water pump in the house.

We went to the dedication of Tiber Dam as it was a very special event. President Truman and his daughter Margaret were there and he pushed the button that blew up the first dirt for the flood control dam. We drove there early in the morning, but there was already a huge crowd. Then we followed the presidential train out of Chester to Shelby where President Truman spoke again. It was a day the students were excused from classes to attend the festivities. We even took a sack lunch for this event. We saw President Truman again when we went with a group of Democrats to Portland, Oregon for the Rose Festival. We got to speak with President Truman! Later, he and his wife Bess led the Parade of Roses.

Electricity:

At first we had a 6-volt generator, so we had electric lights. Then in 1940, we purchased a 32-volt generator and a 32-volt wind generator, also known as a wind charger, with batteries, we also had a propane refrigerator and stove. In 1946, we built a new brick house and purchased a 110-volt gas generator to supply power for the construction.

When the Rural Electric Association, REA, came in 1948, electricity for daily power became a reality. We no longer needed the huge glass batteries which had occupied a little room in the basement of our home. We cleaned several out, and used them for the most wonderful goldfish tanks!

Food:

When we were first married, Mrs. Love gave us lots of garden vegetables and I canned most of this produce. Jack Price gave us a pressure cooker for a wedding present, so I was set up to can. I canned a lot of meat too. When a meat locker became available at Langbell's in town we made good use of it for our meat.

We could butcher a critter, take it into Langbells to be cut up and frozen and stored in our locker box. That was a great help for the ranchers; to be able to use their own fresh meat and not have to can so much. Next, we could have our own freezer at home and consquently, Langbells went out of the locker business.

Our homes:

In 1915, LaVern's parents came from Kansas and located north of Fowler. They first lived in a house built of railroad ties that had been built by the original homesteader, Gene Woodward, a barber in Conrad. They lived there until the Keil brothers built the house in 1916 and a barn. A well was dug a short distance West, so they had to haul water for household use. Livestock either watered at the well or went to the Dry Fork. The water in the wells over on that sand was good as the springs. Just a few miles west everything had too much alkali.

Henry and Florence's home at the East Place.

In 1936, we spent 2 weeks in the cook shack (used as a bunk house) when harvesting out East of Conrad.

In 1934, LaVern moved a 20x20 homestead house (Stattler's) onto a basement on his homestead. At first we hauled water in cans for household use from the reservoir. Later he dug a hole and plastered the dirt sides to form a cistern.

Then LaVern built a porch on the homestead home and in 1942 built on the bedroom with bathroom and garage. We also built the stone barn at this time.

In 1948, we built the brick house. Our family sure was glad to have such a nice home and some space.

In 1974, the little stone shop was torn down and the shop and apartment was built. We moved into it and Dale and Sheri went into the brick house.

Rabbits:

Whoever was running the tractor farming would chase down the baby cottontails and jackrabbits. We had a pen at home where they were put. The kids would play with them. We never ate these rabbits, however we shot young jack rabbits and fried them up for a tasty meal. We never ate the big jackrabbits either, because of the disease, Tularemia.

One time we went to Glen and Esther Hollansworth's East of Brady for a visit during the winter. We took the gun along to shoot jack rabbits. There were a lot of them about. When we got home we had the trunk of the car full of 46 rabbits. LaVern brought them into the basement at the East Place. As they thawed out, he skinned them and stretched the hides on wood frames. He always got lots of fleas from doing this job. He had to strip and take a bath before coming on into the house.

Magpies:

There were lots of magpies, big flocks of them.

It was great sport to rob the magpie nests and do away with the eggs and chicks. We tried to get rid of those rascals because they picked holes into the cattle, especially the brand spot or any sore spot. They would peck at the eyes and feet of the baby calves.

Once when LaVern was a kid, he saw a magpie pecking on the back of a pig, so know what, he got the 22 gun and shot the magpie--and the pig, to his amazement. There was a pig butchering that day.

Over at the old home place, in the winter time, we'd nail rabbits onto the corral posts, and then LaVern would go out into the barn and through a peep hole, shoot the pests while they were dinning on the rabbit. He had to be pretty sly and quiet.

Robbing nests was our best control.

For years, the Puzon and Giskaas families came from Great Falls a couple of weekends a year to rob nests. Our kids never missed a chance. "Whenever riding to check the cattle, we would ride under a magpie nest, stand up on the saddle and rob the nest. They were always in the thorny buffalo berry tree so you wanted to have gloves or a good stick."--Charlotte.

Cream:

In 1936, we milked four cows by hand, separated the milk with a hand crank separator, and sold cream. Sometimes, I made butter if we couldn't get the cream to town. I even made and sold cottage cheese. We also usually had extra eggs to sell.

Many ladies churned and molded butter in one pound bricks. The grocery stores sold these bricks. In the early days, this is where the grocery stores got their butter and cream.

When getting cream to market, the family put the cream can on the wagon, drove the team to Fowler, put the cans on the train. The cans were taken off at Conrad. It was picked up and taken to the creamery in Conrad. The cream cans were returned the same way. Before the Conrad Creamery opened, the cream cans were put on the Fowler train and traveled to Spokane.

Milking cows was very important because the cream check bought our groceries. The extra separated skim milk was added to grain, soaked and fed to the pigs.

Home-made cottage cheese:

Use fresh unpasteurized milk. Set it out in a warm place to clabber (sour), when set up, put on the stove on low heat. It will separate the curds from the whey. Put in a bag and let drain. I usually hung it on the clothesline when nice outside. We mixed it with cream, salt and pepper to serve.

Salad soup (Salat, the German word):

Boiled eggs, green onions, sliced cucumbers, lettuce, salt and pepper. In the old days they just put clabbered milk on for dressing. Now when I make it I use buttermilk and cream for the dressing. Sometimes I use sour cream if I have it.

Friends - Phillipinos:

Smile and Angel came to the ranch and would hunt jack rabbits-Pops would feed one a day to the chickens. They were in the area for many years doing odd jobs and yard work in Conrad.

In the 60s, a group of Philippine students had a scholarship to attend school in Michigan. They came to Montana to visit their Uncle Angel. The county agent was shocked at the shape Angel's house was in, so a place for them to stay had to be found. The county agent knew we were friends of Angel, so we became hosts to the students. They cooked native dishes for us and were wonderful guests.

At that time, Don and Kay were here in the yard and Helen was tiny. The students enjoyed Helen because she looked like one of their brown babies. They made wonderful babysitters. One day LaVern took them to open the ice for the cows. They were afraid, never having driven or walked on frozen water.

Angel always read everyone's palms. He did a lot of yard work in the area after the Conrad Hotel closed. He always called LaVern, 'Vernee'. He was always in the Whoop-Up parade.

Angel worked for Mrs. Reaves who owned the Conrad Hotel and restaurant in the 30's. He got four other Pilipino boys to come. They came out to the ranch with Leviene and a friend. The boys were avid Tennis players and as a result, a tennis court was built at the ranch. These boys bought a convertible car and when driving back from Glacier Park —too fast- rolled that convertible over and killed the four of them. Smile was not with them that day as he was working that day. He went to high school in Conrad and became a family friend. He became a pilot and flew in WWII. He would stop in every now and then.

Mae and Lawrence Able's little girl was about 2 or 3 years old when she died. Mae was washing clothes, or perhaps it was for the floor. She had a bucket of scolding water and the little girl backed up to the bucket and fell in.

Uncle Lawrence was a ditch rider. In his younger days, it was said he took wild horses to Canada and sold them. Some of the horses belonged to ranchers, as they would turn them loose for the winter. Most of the horses were wild mustangs. This was one way for young men to make money in those lean years. There was a good market for horses with the Mounties in Canada.

This sad story happened when Esther Hollandsworth's sister, Loretta, was a teenager. Most girls had one wool skirt and two wool sweaters for school. On weekends, they would wash them in gas. It was winter and she brought the gas inside to warm it up on the stove. It exploded and burned her to death. Loretta Keil Grubb is named for this Loretta.

LaVern and I often went to visit Glen and Esther Hollandsworth, who lived east of Brady. Glen and LaVern had attended the Agriculture Short Course at Bozeman together. LaVern learned to swim at Glen's urging. One should always be able to save yourself.

They always argued about whose tractor could pull the most, and which was best, cattle or sheep. So, one day, LaVern loaded up the Keils Case tractor on the old Reo truck and off to the Hollandsworths we went. Lavern and his wheel tractor, and Glen with his Cat, tore up the fields all afternoon. Mr. Hollandsworth was out on the hills

LaVern and Glen Hallensworth.

herding sheep watching "such darn foolishness."

One day, Glen and LaVern decided to see if the Ford coupe we owned could make it up the East Knees Butte. So off we went and didn't quite make it up to the top, but dug up some dirt.

We went out to Hollandsworth's when their son, Harvey, was born. Glen told LaVern he'd better get more practice in as we had two girls and no boy. Well, a year later, Donald was born--it must have worked--and Dale was next.

Glen was shot by a drunken hired man in 1948, so ended a wonderful friendship LaVern and Glen had. Esther is still one of our most treasured friends.

The family came home and Glen noticed the light was on in the basement of the house. He went downstairs to investigate, and the hired man was hiding and shot Glen with a rifle he had taken from Glen's home. The family heard the shot; Harvey was shot in the hand. Esther grabbed the baby and hid him in the trees. The man was caught and spent many years in jail.

Chapter 5
Rattlesnakes

Rattlesnakes:

When Tiber Dam was built, many rattlesnakes moved up river. There are lots of rattlesnakes all along the breaks. There was a den just south of Fowler on the west side of the road, and we often checked it out.

I saw my first rattlesnake under some old boards by the corral gate. I could hardly get the milk cows in that night and I wondered why and finally heard the rattler. I went and got a hoe and cut him into so many pieces he was almost hash. I ended up being able to skin and tan their hides and made some really nice exhibits and gifts. I also cooked up some of the rattlesnake loin;

About 1980 I finally got to tanning rattlesnake hides, tried frying the loin. It was good and it tasted a lot like lobster. The loin is a small strip that you fillet off. One person holds the head end and another holds the tail end and the body is still wiggling after the snake has been killed. Fry the loin in butter.

As time went on we had many experiences with snakes. We came across snakes as we rode horses checking cattle. One must always watch around gate posts, and never pick up an irrigation pipe by the end. When picking up bales in the field, bales were always rolled toward you in case there was a snake under it. We always had to watch around the stacked grain. Charlotte and I were riding when our Pinto stopped dead because he was right over a rattler. I pulled several out of holes with a barbed wire. They come out fighting mad. Once I got three out of the same hole. I killed them with a hoe or rocks or whatever was handy. I even took the stays out of a wire gate because there was no other wire around. In 2007 Dale stopped, having seen a rattler coiled by the side of the road. Upon inspection, we saw he was eating a gopher. The snake had the gopher in as far as its shoulders. We didn't have a camera, so we ran home to get one. I wished we had waited to see how long it would take to swallow the gopher.

Once going down blackberry coulee chasing cattle with Jennifer we saw a pair of snakes mating. They were hiding under sagebrush.

LaVern knew all about rattlesnakes, as he grew up with them. He knew how to watch for them and beware, how to watch for holes by gateposts, to never pick up a pipe by the end, beware of lumber and post piles, rock piles, shady places out of the sun, and not to mess around holes.

It is neat to run a barbed wire down a gopher hole that a snake had just gone down. They really come out on the fight, so you have your shovel ready. Once three snakes came out of the same hole. One time Dale and LaVern were walking thru the trees. It was pretty cool out. Snakes are slow when it is cold. Dale looked and there LaVern was standing on a rattler not even knowing it. For a minute Dale couldn't speak, then he called, "Stand still, Dad, rattlesnake!" Guess they made short work of that one.

LaVern, with Loretta at 6 or 7 years old, was working under the combine cutter bar for quite some time. Finally, the rattler must have got tired of the noise and put out his warning. It was very close by, but it stayed coiled while they got a ways off.

And did you ever dig the weeds and junk out of a plugged up duckfoot and grab a hold of one of those wiggly fellows. Sort of gets you a bit excited. One time LaVern and Loretta, she was about 5, were going to the old barn to milk the cows and there was one coiled up right by the path.

The snakes were plentiful along the Marias and the North end of the Dry Fork. Hardly ever found any 2 or 3 miles west or south of home. After Tiber Dam was built, the snakes seemed to be more plentiful as the water flushed them out of their holes and they came up river.

A person had to be careful when they went out poisoning gophers. This came to mind when once a rattler came from behind me, passed me and went down his hole. That will make you freeze over.

LaVern once stepped on a rattler going down a hole, then he had a problem, the head and the tail were out of the hole and he needed help, hollered and somebody came with a shovel. What most people don't know is that when a rattler crawls into a hole, his head and tail are at the mouth of the hole for protection, ready for action.

When you pick up a hay bale in the field, you always lifted it towards yourself and stepped back. Rattlesnakes would often times go under anything so they could be out of the sun.

Once I met, well actually, ran over a rattler with the car, on the road. The snake had been cut up into pieces 6 inches long, after I ran back and forth over it with the car, I got out of the car and got ready to step on the head to smash it good, the bugger struck with that short of a piece of body. It struck the toe of my open toed shoes. That straightened things out in a big way. Since then I have had a great

Vivian holds the skins of rattle snakes that she had tanned.

deal of respect for rattlers, every piece and part, whole or not.

Two people were bit on the ranch by rattlers: One was Tom Grey, while he was out poisoning gophers; he stuck his hand down a gopher hole to see how dry the hole was. Well to his surprise, there was a visitor and he got his finger bit. We rushed him to the town doctor, and he recovered.

The second bite was when Makes Coldweather was out changing irrigation pipe. A rattler struck and got hung up on his pant leg. He reached down to grab the enemy, and when he did, the snake came loose and struck his hand. He killed the snake and then took off for the doctor. He was pretty sick for a few days but made an uneventful recovery.

Cloudy, our gray gelding was bitten on the nose by a rattlesnake. He was a nice young gray. It started swelling shut and because a horse could not breathe through its mouth, he was in dire straits. He stood straddle legged and gave us a "please help me" look. We called the vet who gave him a steroid shot, and the swelling went right down, and he lived.

There were lots of black (bull) snakes here. It was easy to tell the difference and we never killed them. For many years, we never saw a gopher on the ranch, maybe thinning out the snakes let them increase, as they could eat two or three gophers.

Down on the Dry Fork Dale saw a bull snake harassing a goose and goslings. He caught the snake and let it go up on the wheat strips. The next day, same place, caught another one by the goose. He moved that one too.

We were messing around the buffalo kill and there was a "small 12 inch" snake hiding under some buffalo bones. It being cold and stiff, I was able to scoop it up into two telescoping paper cups. On the way home, the snake warmed up and was protesting. You could hear him rattling in there. LaVern got a gallon glass jug and I was going to drop snakey into it. Coming out alive, well, and protesting, LaVern moved out of danger and the snake fell on the floor. We were in the shop. We finally got him corralled again in the jar. Dale took him to grade school for show and tell where the snake would strike from within the jar. Then he went on to the high school science class. They pickled him and had him on display for a long time.

When picking rocks the men found a nest of small rattlers. I skinned and tanned one of them. He had just one tiny button for a rattle.

Tanning Recipe:

I decided to try tanning snakeskins having learned that glycerin would preserve and keep the skins nice and pliable.

I would split the snake down the belly with scissors and could just pull the skin right off. Usually I got someone to hold the dead snake with pliers (on the head end but the head had been cut off); I had to be very careful to keep the rattles on the hide. Then I would wash the hide in soapy water and carefully scrape the fat and residue off the skin. Next, I stretched the hide on a beaverboard, with scale side down, and pinned it with stickpins to hold it firm.

For about six days, I rubbed glycerin onto the hide. On taking the skin off the board, I placed the skin on paper towels and rolled them up to keep them in shape and store them. They came out nice and soft, and nice to handle. Some of them Charlotte helped me nail to boards with decorative braids for display.

I tanned many of them for the pipe changers and gifts. The longest one was about 6 feet long and the shortest one was only a foot long with only a tiny button.

The interesting thing is after the snake head is off and the skin is off, the heart will continue to beat an hour or so and the body continues to twist around.

Chapter 6
Arrow Heads

Arrow Heads:

The first arrowhead was found here on our place where the soil blew off the powdered sandy summer fallow fields and around gates. This was in the 1920's and on. Moms had found a few, and LaVern found a few on Grandpa's and Pops' place in the sand. We had found several and were showing them to people and carelessly left them out, and they were stolen. Then we began to watch more closely and found more. There was a buffalo kill on the Marias River north of the Jarvis place. We looked around the rows of Pishkins rocks (the rows of rocks the Indians hid behind) while the buffalo were being chased toward the buffalo kill. When the Marias River was low, we could look below the buffalo kill. Bones were all along the cliff above the river, along the river and on the banks. We would find bones, big skulls and some arrowheads. I think the girls looked there too. The 1948 and 1964 floods washed that buffalo kill bank all away. We kept looking every chance at the area of where the top soil blew off. Down toward Ledger was a good place to hunt for arrowheads too.

Mr. Crawford, whom we met at a Farmers Union Camp on Birch Creek, took us up onto the Two Medicine where a buffalo kill was and showed us how to sift, with screens, through the bones and dirt to find arrowheads. Then we went back there several times with our own screens and got the fever and screened

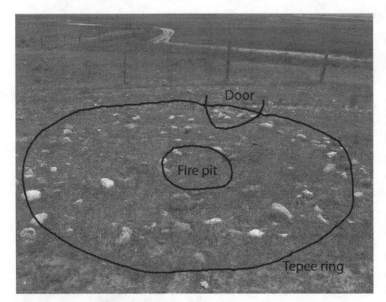

Tepee rings near the buffalo kill.

one of our buffalo kill on our place. In 1934, we took up blade farming so there was less soil loss during the windy periods.

We had heard though the grape vine that Evertt Grigsby, while hunting, had found a buffalo kill on our land. It was on the north side of the Cassidy homestead. So we investigated and began sifting there.

Alice and Vernon and other friends found arrow heads every time they went there. I looked over several spots, finding pieces where evidently Indians made arrowheads. I watched cattle trails, gate sites, road ruts, and blowholes where dirt blows off. Once at Pops' place after a big blow in the strips we found lots of arrow heads. Once we even found a bead and some scrapers. That spring, I was cultivating ahead of

LaVern as he drilled. When I came to a blown place I would stop and looked and found about 40 small arrowheads and one large one, what a thrill.

We have found a number of hammers while picking rocks, and even while checking some rock piles That

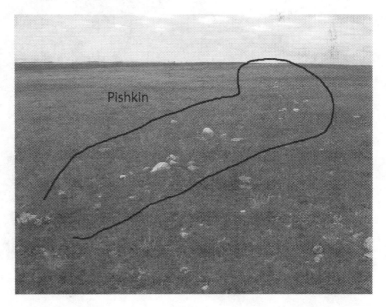

had been dumped on the hillside. We have a couple bowls the Indians used to grind up various things in, as well as a grinding stone. We have also found one large rock the Indians tied horses to, and also some hide scrapers. Charlotte and I are called the "Bent Over Keil Women."

Vivian choosing a site to dig at the buffalo kill.

Vivian & Charlotte at the buffalo kill.

Chapter 7
Railroads

Train wrecks:

Various trains wrecked on the Burlington Northern track bordering our ranch. What follows is a brief history of some of those wrecks.

In 1890, the narrow gage railroad from Great Falls to Lethbridge was built. This did away with most of the Whoop-Up trail travel. Before that wool, pigs, or any salable item had to be hauled or driven to Fort Benton.

In 1930, some railroad car gas tanks rolled over at the South side of the Marias River. Farmers drove around the river with barrels and buckets to retrieve some of this precious liquid. LaVern did get four or five fifty-five gallon barrels. Soon no one could get any as it was too dangerous because of the risk of fire or explosion.

In the early 1920's an apple train wrecked north of Fowler. It was called the apple wreck since there were several cars of apples. Everyone who found out about the wreck came and retrieved apples. This was a wintertime wreck and it so happened it was chinooking, a warm thawing wind. Homesteaders canned apples, made apple butter and dried them. LaVern would not eat any apple dish for several years. He had had his fill of apples.

In 1936, South of Fowler a train with empty cars wrecked at Burk siding.

Floods on the Dry Fork in the 1948 and 1964 took out the railroad tracks and the vehicle bridge across the Dry Fork. After the later flood, the bridge at Fowler was not replaced and now one must ford the creek. Burlington Northern hired our Caterpillar to do work after the 1964 flood.

As told by Loretta: "In August of 1991 there was a head on collision of a Southbound #602 Burlington Northern full grain freight train and a Northbound #603 Burlington Northern lumber and propane tank freight train out of Great Falls. The collision took the lives of three crewmen, and injured other crew members who jumped clear of the trains seconds before the collision."

It was a very hot day. I was riding my white horse, Tar Baby, helping move our cows from the east side of the railroad tracks to Mrs. Norton's pasture on the west side near Fowler. Mark and Erling were beginning to start a few cows underneath the railroad bridge when the train whistle blew. Kristi, my granddaughter, was riding a four-wheeler with her dad, Mark Grubb, and had been waving at the engineer as the train passed the herd of cows. Erling, my husband, was riding his buckskin gelding. I had been up on top the breaks bringing a small bunch of cows down toward the Dry Fork where the main bunch of cows were gathered.

As I watched the front of the train disappear through "the cut", I heard a screeching ripping sound and looked north to see a huge mushroom-like cloud of heavy smoke rise above the hill that hid the front half of the train. As it was the time of the Persian Gulf War, I thought a bomb or something like that had exploded on the train. I hurried my horse down the hill with my heart beating hard.

Suddenly Mark saw a catastrophe of some sort had happened. Mark and Kristi zipped up over the hill to see the two

Grain cars spill their loads.

trains that had hit head on, on the single track. Smoke and fire rolled into the sky. Mark roared toward his house to call 911 and get help. It was an awful sight. The engines reared up against each other with grain cars scattered and spilled every which way.

Erling left his horse at the trailer, unhooked the pickup and drove along the track to get to the wreck on the East side of the track. Erling ran along the track and met a bum who had caught a ride on the train. Mark had returned and he met an engineer trying to find his crew. Neighbors were arriving with firefighting equipment, trying to stop the fire creeping up the hills. Soon after the Shelby fire truck arrived to help.

On the West side of the wreck, the Keil harvest crew had seen smoke and headed down with a water truck. They met two railroad engineers, one badly burned. Dad (LaVern) gave him his shirt. Another man who had been riding the rails showed up too.

The ambulance finally arrived at the accident scene as they had waited up the hill to get clearance to go near the train.

I finally abandoned the cattle drive and rode over to the wreck. Many vehicles were trying to find their way down to the wreck as it was very rugged country. The emergency responders stayed through the night trying to find the railroad crew and keep the fire controlled. Vivian Keil and Evelyn Bruce were two of the area women who organized lunches and delivered them to the wreck site.

The day after, Kristi was interviewed by the "local," fifty miles away, television station. The sheriff organized horseback riders to search the hills for the missing railroad men. As I recall they were found buried in the spilled grain.

Some of the families of the missing railroad men came down to urge the searchers to keep looking. I saw them standing on the railroad track as loaders, caterpillars, and men with shovels were looking – looking – searching. I thought of the song "Down in the Valley." My heart was sad for the families. We "lived" the train wreck for at least two weeks. We would go down every evening to look and think how did this ever happen. It was such an unbelievable sight.

Apparently, miscommunication between a train crew and a Seattle dispatcher was the cause according to the National Transportation Safety Board.
Earlier that very morning, LaVern, Vivian, Charlotte and Gwen had just brought the Keil cattle herd out of that very pasture that was now littered with the smoldering remnants of the two trains."

Other train wrecks that happened near the Ranch:

In 1998 at the Fowler elevator, six cars derailed.
Around 2000, a train load of French fries, also one lumber train.
Additionally, there were two train wrecks at the Marias river bridge.
In 2001, one mile north of Ledger on Jones land several cars left the track.
The Great Northern bought out the Great Falls-Canadian railroad and built the standard tracks on the right of way and straightened most of the right of way, putting a lot of the track on the east side of the Dry Fork. Standard railroad tracks are 56.5" wide because the English built the first railroads. The same builders that built the tramways used the same jigs and tools that they used to build wagons. Wagons were built the width they were because the older roads had ruts just that width, 56.5". When they built wagons that did not fit in the ruts, the wheels readily broke. The width of the old ruts was this distance, because the Romans built the roads in 54 BC to accommodate their wagons and chariots. The Roman wagons and

chariots were 56.5" wide, because that was the equal width of two standard Roman horses. Isn't history wonderful!

There were many crossings on the Dry Fork so the cut was dug through the hill north of Fowler using horse drawn dump wagons. We enjoy hunting for fossils in the cut hillside. We drive through the cut to go north of Fowler on the east side of the tracks.

One of the main uses of the railroad was to haul coal and coke south from the Lethbridge area as well as our area farm products like wool, livestock and grain crops.

We still have a bit of the old narrow gage right-of-way left. For several years they left a third track on the standard track so the narrow gage engine and cars could still haul freight.

The narrow gage railroad, which only had a span of 36", came through from Conrad to Fowler along the Dry Fork in the 1890's. The track reached from Lethbridge Canada to Great Falls and was constructed and run by the North Western Coal and Navigation Company. It was primarily built to haul coal from Canada to the smelter in Great Falls. The section of the railroad in Montana was incorporated under the name of Great Falls and Canadian Railway Company. The railroad was sometimes called the Galt narrow gauge and popularly known as the Turkey Tracks. In 1901, the Great Northern Railway Company purchased the line and converted it into standard gauge, however the third rail was left in place so the narrow gauge could still operate until 1912.

Because the railroad followed the Dry Fork, it was decided to build a railroad cut through a hill north of Fowler, eliminating more creek bridges. Farmers hired out their horses and wagons to haul the dirt out of the cut making the railroad right of way. This construction project helped out the farmers financially since they provided the manpower, horses and equipment. While building the cut, a new man on a flat car fell or jumped off and was killed. During the project Fowler became a thriving headquarters for the construction crews.

At one time, there were two passenger trains each way and the freight trains hauling coal from Canada as well as moving livestock and grain to market. There was a two-story station house for the section crew and a full time depot agent. A person could get on the train in Fowler and ride to Conrad for $.25. Farmers could ship 10-gallon cans of cream from Fowler to Spokane.

John Stein was the depot agent and his wife was a teacher at the Fowler school. Grain was hauled down by team and wagon to the Rocky Mountain elevator at Fowler. Farmers that lived some distance from Fowler would deliver their grain to the elevator and stay overnight in rooms that were above the Fowler store. They would play poker and drink home brew. The horses would be put up at the livery barn. The last elevator manager was Bill Zimmerman. The elevator was dismantled in 2001 after standing idle for many years.

Burlington Northern north of the Marias River.

Chapter 8
How the ranch grew

Land:

We purchased the Jake, John and Leslie Keil homesteads. We also bought the Ed Moore and Pops' homesteads. LaVern also bought Reinhardt Keil's original place from John and August Keil.

Keil Ranch, 1954.

LaVern and I formed a partnership of Keil Ranch on January 1, 1953. In 1967, the Keil's formed a corporation and did some estate planning. We gave land to Loretta, money to Charlotte, land to Donald and ranch stock to Dale. This was done over a five-year period because of gift regulations.

In 1972, Keil Ranch, Inc., sold the August Keil irrigated land to Donald Keil and the Linderman and Pierce places to Newton Conklin. The corporation added the following lands: the Ovens pasture in 1970; the Campbell's land in 1973; the Norton's land in 1979; the Iverson pasture across the Dry Fork in 1983; the Myers land in 1985; and the McCracken pasture along with the leased State land in 1989.

While actively working outside driving the tractor and other farm equipment, except for the combine and Caterpillar, I was also the bookkeeper.

Since 1935, I have cooked for the crews, herded cattle, drove trucks and tractors to summer fallow or for the pull combine, and baled hay when we would bale hay for shares on neighbors' irrigated lands.

In 1977, I became the general manager with Dale as assistant manager. This was in preparation for Social Security as LaVern was nearing 65!

As they became available, we bought up many of the homesteads: land from Toole and Pondera Counties that had been taken over for delinquent taxes, relinquishments, banks, etc. Gus Keil in 1938; George Williams' land in 1939; Stattler; Marsh land in 1946 (a teacher); Rheinhardt Keil; Leslie Keil in 1935; John Keil; Jake Keil; Gordon Morrison, Len Howell, Hudson, Ed Moore (married to Amelia Keil). Pop's place (Henry Keil), and Fred and Grandma Flickinger both in 1947; Fred Sund's land in 1959, also known as the Pearson and Linderman land; Jarvis, Sam Solid, Russel Myers land, and August Keil irrigated land in 1960.

Trees:

LaVern started planting the shelterbelt west of the house in 1934. In later years, the children hoed the weeds in the shelterbelts. Next, we planted the shelterbelt by the East Place for soil conservation and for windbreaks for the cattle.

In 1991, we participated in the Pheasants Forever Project with the Fish and Game Department. We planted hundreds and hundreds of trees, hoed between them by hand, and cultivated between the rows. Many of the original trees are still living. The most hardy and long lived were the Russian Olive, Caragana, and Green Ash.

Rocks:

If you have wondered about the piles of rocks over the hill slopes, this is how they were established. First we used horse and wagons, then the Model T truck. We put sideboards on, picked the rocks out of the ground with a hand pick, loaded them up and hauled them to the first hillside. We drove sideways as close to the edge of the coulee as we dared, took off the sideboard and then kicked and rolled the rocks off. Later, we used the rocks for riprap on reservoir banks, washouts in coulees, and riprap on the Dry Fork banks. What a treat when we got hoists on the trucks. Many loads of rocks were picked before we broke up the land in 1938, and we are still picking them. Most of these piles of rocks were later picked up and moved to the reservoir banks. A bucket

Dumping rocks.

Picking rocks.

tractor was most helpful.

About the last rocks LaVern and I picked together was in the late 1990's. We took a pickup out and loaded it about half full. We took those rocks and rocked the trails going down to the river. We went out about an hour or so every day. Even in our late 80s we still were doing a job together, as always.

Buildings:

In 1940, the stone barn was built using fieldstones; sand and gravel were hauled from the Dry Fork and Marias River. This all had to be shoveled on and off by hand as at that time we had a Model-A truck. The stone were hand-laid on the barn walls-pouring cement to hold them in place. Moms, Pops, Loretta, Charlotte, all helped. Uncle Laurence Able did the carpentry work. He worked for the Valier Reservoir Co. as a ditch rider in the summer and helped us in the winter.

In 1943 or 1944, an addition on the original homestead house was built--a bedroom, bathroom and garage. Before this we had a very fancy three hole out house located between the house and barn. It was mighty cold in the winter.

The Brick House:

In 1948, we built the brick house. Leo Sigety was the main boss of the job. His wife, Irene, LaVern's cousin, lived in the little two-room house we had. Irene helped cook. Vic Heinitz was the head masonry cement and hod (mud between bricks) carrier for the bricklayer. He did all of the mixing. The bricklayer had trouble being at

The stone barn, built from field stone & cement. Big hay mow had hard wood floor. Many dances were held in it when it was empty.

work due to the whisky bottle. I found the whisky bottle, emptied it out and filled with water and Tabasco sauce. "It sure did help!" Ray and Marge Heinitz lived at the East Place and worked for us. The average number of people we cooked for was 12. The house got built of bricks so there was no painting. Radiant

Yard showing original home, barn, chicken house, hired man's house in background. Note the wind charger for power.

heat was a new discovery so we put that in along with two fireplaces. It was so cozy all the time.

The kids learned lots of cuss words from Leo while trying to help with the building.

Once we had to improvise when the electricity was off for a week after a terrible blizzard. We cooked on a two-burner gas camp stove, bailed water out of the cistern, and kept the fireplace burning. Florence (my sister) had been out to visit that weekend. After three days, the men, with shovels finally got her back to town. It took all day.

In 1938, we built a shop out of cement and rocks that LaVern and I had picked from the fields. Later, the cribbed granary, the half-round livestock shed and the Butler Building were built.

In 1973, the stone shop was torn down and we built the new shop and apartment. We had to tear down the old stone shop. It was no longer large enough and we needed to improve the situation. After taking the roof off, they knocked the walls down and hauled pieces off. LaVern jumped up on the truck bed to shift a chunk of the dismantled wall, when all of a sudden, it fell apart. LaVern lost his balance and fell backwards, hitting his head on the edge of the truck bed. Knowing he was hurt bad, we called the ambulance. X-rays showed he had nearly broken his neck. After ten days in the hospital, hanging by his head with a traction device, he was able to go home with his chin resting on a neck brace and a back brace. He could not be without the braces day or night for six weeks. He could not turn his

Keil Ranch, Conrad, Montana

head, bend or nod, however, he could do anything else he wanted. One of the jobs we had during this period was to build a mile of fence to the east. Dennis Grigsby drove the posts and set the ties. Working together LaVern and I rolled out the wire. He did this while in his braces. Eventually LaVern graduated to just a neck collar, and that was for a long time.

In 1949, the butler building was built. A seed cleaning room was set up in the south end. Many crops of grass seed and registered grain seed was cleaned here. The seed cleaning process would last throught the winter. The hay storage was under the expansive lean-to that was built on the east side of this building, adjacent to the corrals.

Crib grainery; it was later sided with tin.

The Barn:

We had three or four barn dances in the new stone barn built in 1942 before hay was put in the hayloft. The loft has a nice smooth hardwood floor. Who ever played a musical instrument in the community came and played for the dances.

"Mrs. Munson had come from Fowler to baby sit us kids. I awoke and wondered outside to see where Mom and Dad were. I walked

1. Original house
2. Brick house
3. Stone shop
4. Married hired man's house
5. Bunk house
6. Butler building
7. Barn
8. Outhouse
9. Chicken house
10. Pig shed
11. Crib grainery
12. Equipment storage
13. Cattle shed
14. Hay storage

Keil Ranch, Conrad, Montana, 1954.

Red grainery.

over to the barn to see all the activity. People were playing cards in the calf pen and ladies were serving sandwiches in the oat bin. I felt so important when Dad picked me up and danced with me. I was 4 years old. I spent many wonderful hours in that barn."--Charlotte.

The barn was used to milk cows in, feed 4-H calves, and later for the bulls to winter in.

"I love our big barn. It was a huge part of my young life. The cows were milked there. I always went with Dad evenings. The cats hung around, waiting for him to squirt milk in their mouths. The horses had two stalls. I loved the sound of them stomping and blowing their noses, eating, and I loved the smells—the animals and the hay."--Loretta

Pops brought some of his special fossil rock and cut, polished rocks to lay in the wall of the barn by the walk-in door. He was pretty proud to see them on display.

We also built a red grainery for additional grain storage. It was a wooden building and was always painted red. We used this for grain storage.

Cattle:

Blackleg:

LaVern's 4-H club project was a dairy calf. Blaine Ferguson, the county agent, knew of Guernsey calves out of Tillamook, Oregon. He ordered some for the boys to use as their 4-H projects. Imagine LaVern's dismay when he found his heifer calf dead from blackleg. But worst of all, the magpies were pecking her eyes out.

Hereford cattle watering at the well on East Place; 1985.

We also had three dead steers from blackleg. These were 2-year-old steers, as we never sold calves. When moisture came, the blackleg bug was activated. Somehow we had missed vaccinating them. That bug is always there. I know we never waited too long to vaccinate the calves at that time.

Where I grew up, there was no blackleg or vaccination for it. This disease was new to me. We had taken John Bill's cattle in on pasture and put them down into Grandpa's pasture. Checking them after a long wet spell, we found a few dead from blackleg. John had never vaccinated for that. We moved them out and all got shots. After that only once can I remember losing any of our cattle from blackleg; we must have been careless or forgot one.

Mr. Hollandsworth was along when LaVern went back to St. Paul with cattle. They got $400 for the carload. When LaVern questioned the small check, the buyer said, "You should have been here yesterday-a man came in with carload of sheep and did not get enough to pay the freight. He owed money instead of getting some." This was in 1934.

Then, they went on to Chicago to the World's Fair for a few days and had a good time. About ready to get on the train to come home, LaVern was out of money, so at the café he ate bread and more bread. I hope nearly enough to get him home before starving. I think Mr. Hollandsworth must have treated him once in a while to get home.

Mr. Hollandsworth told many times of LaVern running out of money the last day and stuffing himself with free bread.

We sold a couple of our cattle for $36 to a cattle buyer by the name of Blake. He had a little trailer and a tiny sales yard in Conrad.

When we homesteaded, there were predominately Shorthorn and Hereford cattle available in the area. We bought some Hereford cows from Mr. Blake, the local cattle buyer. We also bought Hereford bulls, our first from Stanford, Montana. We also bought some Hereford bulls from a breeder at Choteau.

When Pops got ready to sell cattle, they gathered up a carload and drove them to Shelby. Once they got to the Marias River, it was very high and they could not get the cattle started across. Finally, one old cow started across and they got the cattle all across and drove them on up the Shelby coulee and to the stockyards where they were loaded onto stock rail cars. The owners could ride in the caboose free, taking their own bedroll and food. The owners liked to see that the cattle were taken care of. The cattle were unloaded at least twice for feed and drink on the way to Chicago or St. Paul. The owners got a free ticket home.

For years when we had dry pastures, we would have to haul water out to the cows. Then the Tiber water came when the military put in lines from Tiber Dam to a training site south of Conrad. That project was dropped and the farmers and ranchers organized and finished the Tiber water project. This made water available to all of us. We even had enough for household, livestock and some yard irrigation.

One year we had a two-headed calf stillborn on the ranch. It had two mouths and noses, four eyes and three ears. I skinned the head carefully and boiled the skull. After long hours of work, I had the calf head mounted and it was very lifelike. We still have that specimen and to this day, our great grandchildren take it to school for show and tell.

We always kept forty plus replacement heifers from the previous calf crop to replace any culled cows. We wintered them at the home place.

Every spring brought the two-day roundup of the herd and branding of the new calves. Many of the family members and friends would converge at the East Place where the nice corrals and sheds were. The first day the horses and riders would gather the herd and bring them to the small pasture next to the East Place. Since the cows were fed all winter from a pickup, the cows would usually follow it to the small pasture after they had been gathered from the breaks. The second day, the cows and calves were driven into the corral and would be separated. The calves would be vaccinated for blackleg, branded, dehorned and castrated, if necessary. I was careful to save the Rocky Mountain oysters and would prepare them for that evening's meal. I kept the books and would choose which calves we would keep as bulls. The cows were worked through the chute to be administered insecticide and checked for health. Everyone worked hard, had a job and were all rewarded with a great picnic meal in the shade of the shed. I would always prepare this picnic fare the day prior to the branding day. When finished, the horses and riders would take the herd to nearby fresh pastures.

LaVern working the cattle at East Place.

We got excited about registered cattle seeing them at the fairs and some of our friends had some. We bought the first ten registered cows from Wayne Hill at Drummond. At this time, we also had about 125-quality grade Herefords.

We also bought some registered stock from the Driesen's of Cut Bank. One of these cows lived to a great ripe old age and she was a great lead cow. She always knew to lead the herd in the right direction when we moved them.

We did show and sell some of our registered Hereford bulls at the Shelby Hereford bull sale sponsored by the Montana registered Hereford Association. We got acquainted with some wonderful area ranchers. We have remained lifetime friends. We sold a lot of quality calves to local 4-H members. They won many blue ribbons and championship trophies with our calves.

Branding before the chutes were built.

The feeder market changed and those buyers preferred crossbred calves to finish. We tried crosses using Mury Grey, Semintal, Red and Black Angus, and

Vivian working the cattle at East Place during branding.

Charlois bulls. The best cross with our good Hereford cows was with the Black Angus bulls. The Herefords had superior disposition and milk, the Angus gave good hybrid vigor and good performance in the feedlot.

Loretta and Charlotte often went to check on cattle and fix fencing on horseback. Before the girls took over these chores, I spent a lot of time checking cattle in the summer, as well as moving bulls around, changing pastures, etc. The girls were also a big help in the house with cooking.

LaVern and I calved until 1997, and for 12 years, we did the major part of the calving work. Before then, we drove over and checked on our calving program almost every day. Before 1993, LaVern, the crew and I handled most of the bales by hand feeding the cattle. In the 1990's during calving season, LaVern and I stayed over at the East Place barn.

Until recently, we would spend two months calving out the cows plus fixing fence and moving cattle and general fetch-it jobs.

For years we climbed a ladder to get to our little bunk house in the barn/corrals. The kids decided I was getting too old to climb the ladder with jugs of water and supplies, so a stairway was built. A family of owls nested on top of our little home. In the night we would hear "scratch, scratch" and "hoot hoot" for hours. We finally closed that area so, "no more owls". Charlotte came and kept us company a few nights.

LaVern and Vivian in back. Boxer breeding Hereford bull. Donald on bull.

We had one calf with severe scours. It was so bad I decided just pills would not do and I needed to go to the vet. The van would have to make the trip. I had a big cardboard box to put in the back. We caught the little bugger by hand and got it into the box. Charlotte managed to keep the calf contained in that open-top box for the trip to the vet and back to the pasture. Good luck so far!

Just as I was lifting the calf out of the box to release it to the waiting anxious mom, it let loose and pooped - lots of loose poop - all over. Luckily a good share stayed in the box, but the calf had begun to struggle and had flattened part of the box. The van required a big clean up job - it was worth it, as the calf survived!

We were happy living in our one-room abode. Someone decided that the hired help needed better accommodations, so an extra room with a proper bathroom and an improved calving pen were built on.

LaVern and I improved the corrals for the calving operation by putting up a pole barn with a full length feed bunk, water fountain, lights, vet room, indoor hay shed, and a bunk house upstairs in the barn. I stocked the place with soups, hot drinks etc. We stayed most nights watching the expectant moms. We assisted births, milked out big bags, grafted orphan calves, whatever had to be done. It was really fun and we enjoyed it.

These corrals are located at the East Place because it was ideal for calving out. There were small sandy pastures and water fountains complimented with trees that formed shelterbelts providing protection from the weather.

I complained about walking the 100 or so feet to the outhouse in the cold weather. So—LaVern and I pulled that toilet inside the pole barn—he called that my "indoor toilet." Later on, a proper bathroom was built. At least the hired help got to enjoy it.

Branding was always an eventful day. First, we had to gather the cattle in to the East Place. Using horses and pickups and in the later years, four wheeled all terrain vehicles, we would bring the cattle up from pasture to a smaller pasture next to the east place. The evolution of using ATVs to herd the cattle got the boys involved, as they were not really horse lovers.

Before we got the new pole barn up with the calf chute, the men grabbed a calf then wrestled it to the ground. We heated the branding irons using a campfire until we got electricity, then we used electric irons. The brand that represented the Keil ranch is a V on top of an O and is read, V over O. This was originally Dad's (Matt Venetz) brand. LaVern's first brand was bar lazy KL.

There was calf riding for the kids and bigger animals for the guys. The Puzons, Giskas, Harold Daniels, along with others, and all available family members, and always many other kin came, and we had good crews.

Merle Norton would always participate and would say "By dod me no fall off", but did! LaVern often paid him with silver dollars so he could show off his wages. He lived with his grandmother one and a half miles away and often walked by on his way to Fred Flickinger, his uncle and our neighbor to the south. Everybody liked him.

We would always have a big picnic lunch for the crew. Of course, we would always save the rocky mountain oysters, the calf testicles. I would fry them up in butter and they were quite tasty. For years, the calves were castrated by cutting them, but eventually we used rubbers when the calves were young. This was a lot less work and would not create yet another place that insects could bother the calf. Of course, we always kept some of the nicer calves for bulls, and would make a determination at branding whether to keep them as bulls or make them a feeder calf. There were always a few calves that we would miss with the rubbers, so we would take care of them as well. I always kept the pocket book record of the cows and calves. I would record which cow produced the nicest calves and such. We would cull out cows that lost their calves or did not drop a calf at all that year. They would be sold at the auction or kept for our own consumption.

The cattle were always loaded with flies by that time, so we poured on fly control and put ear tags in the ears. A few times, we had an airplane fly and spray over the watering sites as the flies hatched out in the manure and wet. We hung dust bags around the watering sites as well for insect control. Flies can become annoying for the cattle so ranchers had to use different methods to minimize this. These flies also spread pinkeye so it was very important to control them.

Machinery:

LaVern and I worked together on the ranch. We would get a housekeeper to tend the children in the summer.

I drove the tractor on the pull type combine or sometimes hauled the grain. If I got to daydreaming on the tractor, LaVern threw hands full of grain at me to wake me up.

You should sometime harvest mustard with a pull type outfit-no cabs. You hoped you never sweat or the mustard dust sure got hot. We had several good years raising mustard, and then the market and dry weather took over.

First, we had Gleaner combines-pull type, then a John Deere pull type, followed by Massy Harris self-propelled. What an improvement when self-propelled combines came out in the mid 40's. During the war, machinery was hard to come by.

LaVern bought a John Deere pull type combine in Lewistown. Leviene and Al were living there at that time. I think Al helped locate that one. Aunt Gertrude and Charlotte went with LaVern. The dealer rigged up a hitch for the combine to be towed by the truck.

Pull-type combines. Note the fuel trailer hand pump used for transfer.

About 25 miles out of Lewistown (towing the combine behind a grain truck) a big wheel came off the combine, and it started whipping and tipped over on the highway. The dealer came to help. Most of the damage was bent stuff on the left side. Well, he got the wheel on again and home with it only to find out we'd had a hailstorm, this was about July 1. The remainder of the trip was slower and uneventful; imagine that! The combine did make it to the ranch in time for harvest.

Loretta and Charlotte mowed the crested wheat grass fields with the little Fordson Tractors with the side-

The grain door was dropped on the combine tank and grain ran into the truck/Model L Case, '38 Ford pickup, and Gleaner combine.

mounted mower. They raked the hay with side delivery rakes pulled by Willies jeeps. Loretta went to hay baler school and did most of the hay baling. The hay bales were all picked up by hand, loaded on a trailer and stacked by hand in the hay shed. Hired help did the heavy work and the kids learned to drive the pickup while picking hay. Loretta got so she could stack hay along with the guys.

Loretta, Charlotte, Donald and Dale helped with the cattle and other chores that had to be done. Donald drove the swather, tractor, combine and trucks in addition to helping with the irrigation. All the children drove vehicles hauling hay and picking rocks when they were barely big enough to reach the pedals.

The first self-propelled combine was the Super 90 MF. I ran the tractor often to summer fallow while LaVern was in charge of haying, irrigation, seeding and harvest. I did not run the combine for fear of picking up a rock.

Eventually, in 1944, we bought a Caterpillar tractor and later, another D6 Caterpillar; LaVern did lots of work for neighbors, mostly building reservoirs for $10.00 per hour. These cats also pulled the combines. We put in the reservoirs, for cattle water after we bought the two D6 Caterpillars. These two cats also pulled the drills and did summer fallow. The outfits ran day and night to get all of the work done.

In our lifetime we have watched and participated in the changes in the machinery. When we were kids, everything was horse powered except for the steam engine. The steam engines were used for plowing (the heavier work), the threshing machine and the railroad.

The land was first plowed with a moldboard plow, then disced and harrowed. Next came the disc plow. Needless to say we tried to work the land when it was moist. To summer fallow after the disc plow we used a one-way. It had smaller discs than the disc plow and would really chew up the ground causing lots of blowing fields.

Then Noble of Noble's Ford, Alberta, Canada came up with a blade idea. It was a single blade that went under

Cats building the resevoir east of home place.

the stubble, left the stubble standing, and would result in good ground cover. This pulled very hard. Next, Noble came out with two big duck foot shovels (like sweeps) on the blade. This did a better summer fallow job and pulled much easier.

The next generation of plow that we used was a duck foot and rod weeder combination. By implementing strip farming we did a pretty good job of saving the land from erosion by the wind. Now, chemical summer fallow is being used by farmers.

Seed was planted with single disc drills. Then, we went to a double disc drill with a fertilizer attachment. Now we can seed and fertilize at the same time. The next type of drill had a narrow shovel. Now many farmers use the air drills and seeding and fertilizing can be done at the same time.

Weed control in growing crops is now done with chemicals. Initially we had no way to control weeds in the crops except to seed later, and cultivating the summer fallow.

Harvesting – I remember when grain was cut and elevated into the header wagon then stacked by hand. The threshing machine pulled up alongside the stack and men pitched the crop into the feeder of the threshing machine. The grain was hauled in horse-drawn wagons and hand shoveled into bins. Sometimes these were abandoned homestead shacks. Finally someone developed grain augers. The shacks used for grain bins, had to have the mice and junk cleaned out. We had to make sure that all of the holes had tin over

Duckfoot cultivator with rod weeders behind, D6 Cat, Graham Home cultivator - all hand levers to raise & lower machines.

them so the grain would not run out. In fact the house we first lived in was used for grain storage for a short time by Pops and Grandpa Keil.

After the headers, the binder was developed and would make bundles of grain that were then shocked. A shock was eight to ten bundles of grain that stood upright against one another. It worked to bind the grain when it was not quite ripe and let it ripen in the shock. These bundles would be forked into wagons and taken to the threshing machine. In this area, everyone would watch for rattlesnakes under

Seeding with a double disc drill.

the bundles. Where I grew up south of Conrad, there were no rattlesnakes or bull snakes.

The first threshing machines were powered by steam engines, then later by the farmer's tractors. The first threshing machines were not owned by the farmers, but instead by a crew that would travel around to the farms, threshing their grain, then move to the next farm. The threshing crew usually consisted of the threshing machine man, the engineer that ran the steam engine, a spike pitcher who pitched in the bundles that dropped to the ground as the wagon man would miss the feeder sometimes, six or seven bundle wagons, and a cook car to feed the crew. There was also a flunkey who did whatever, such as haul fuel or water, help the cook and getting groceries. My brother, Vernon did this for quite a few years.

The straw was blown up in big stacks by the thresher machine. The cattle could eat around them in the winter time. It was fun to climb up on the straw pile and slide down or play hide and seek in it, if near the homestead. We almost always had a

Header, binder, making bundles.

stack nearby, as most farms were small. Otherwise the stacks were further out in the field near the shocks so the crew did not have to haul the bundles so far.

Next came the combine. The first

Hauling bundles to the thresher.

Steam engine powering the thresing machine.

little pull-type, we called it the beetle, combined a cutter bar with a threshing machine. Our first combine was a Baldwin. Often I drove the tractor and LaVern operated the combine. If I was not paying attention, he would throw hands full of grain

at me. We also had a John Deere pull type combine. Next came the self-propelled combine, eliminating the need for a tractor and driver. We first had a Massey Ferguson; these were straight cut machines.

Tractor powered thresher.

Spike pitcher.

We could cut the grain first with a swather before it was fully ripe because we feared that we could lose the crop in a hail storm or if the grain was not ripening evenly. By swathing the grain crop it would speed up the ripening process. Then we would pickup the swath with the combines. Of course there was the threat of a fall rain or a high wind that would ruin the swaths. If you do not swath, you have to wait for the grain to ripen in the field down to at least thirteen percent moisture for it to be safe to store in the bin.

The first grain elevators hauled the grain up the tube with a paddle chain. Then there was an air auger, but it cracked too much grain. Then came the auger type of grain auger like what is used now.

Building a straw pile.

I remember when I was a kid, we hauled our grain to Brady with horses. It was a treat to get to ride to town on the wagon. Then Dad hired the Hennemans of Valier to haul the grain to town with their truck. We finally got our own truck. LaVern's parents hauled their grain to Fowler with horse and wagon. I think their first truck was a Rio. Sometimes they would by-pass the elevator and shovel the grain right into a railroad car, set aside on the siding for them. This was after getting a truck.

LaVern and I got a Model A truck and it could haul 100 bushels.

Hay was mowed by side mounted mowers pulled by horses. Dad sharpened the sickle every night on a foot peddle grind stone. The hay was then raked with the dump rake making windrows. Then the hay was picked up with a hay loader, hauled to the stack and pitched off unless you had one of the unloading items like a slide. A slide was used by pulling the hay off of the wagon onto the slide and then onto the stack. We had a pull stacker where the slings full of hay were lifted off the wagon then dumped onto the stack. A person on top of the stack would have to distribute the hay to make a nice stack. The loose hay could be stored in the loft of a barn to prevent spoilage. Then came the balers.

In 1945, we bought two D6 caterpillar tractors and began to build dams and roads. We built many of the neighbors' reservoirs. We had a number 60 scraper for the cats. At one time, LaVern hired two "cat-skinners" who built two reservoirs. One left rather early but Elmer stayed on longer. We took part of his wages to buy his railroad ticket, but when we came back into town, he had cashed in the ticket, drank up the proceeds, and was in jail. He didn't work for us after that. It came to be that most of these men were of rather shady reputations.

Jason Giard and Ted Thomson also ran the Caterpillars. These two men were our best cat skinners. These versatile tractors were also used to pull the pull-

type combines and for all farming. There was no cab, so no heater or air conditioner, just lots of dust, heat, and noise.

Crude Oil:

When burning crude oil in the L Case tractor, one had to drain oil from the oil pan every day

Fuel—we always had enough, we sure were thrifty though.

We could burn crude oil in the Case tractor (high quality and free of sulfur). We would go up northeast of Shelby to the Burwash wells owned by Gus Blaze. He would pump (a hand pump) our 50 gallon barrels full. (I don't remember if there were 30 gallon barrels then). Lots of men hurt their backs lifting these barrels.

Putting hay in the barn with the hay mow with the team of horses providing the power to raise the hay. Filling the hay mow at the Venetz Ranch.

When using crude oil in a tractor, it made oil, so you had to drain oil off the oil pan. Some people used that oil in their cars.

Grains and Hay:

LaVern and Henry Keil doing some road building on their own near Fowler.

The first wheat we sold was for $.34 per bushel. This was the lowest price we ever sold for.

The story of Betzes barley: The brewing companies were busy getting new varieties of malt barley and were interested in all new varieties. Blaine Ferguson, the county agent said that the Betzes barley looked best in the test plots at

Valier. The malt plant did not like the sample because of so many foreign seeds, like wild oats, were in it, so he let LaVern have the sample. The family, along with Alice and Vernon and other family members, sat around the dining table and we hand cleaned that Betzes barley. In November we sent six bushels, about 360 pounds, off to Elmer Emerick in Arizona. He was increasing registered seed for growers for so much an acre. In April he called to say the barley was ready.

LaVern and Uncle John Keil took off with a truck to bring the seed home from Arizona. There was so much seed that they had to sack some of it up and stack

The thresher.

Albert Hedke threshing on the Fowler place.

The first rubber tired Case tractors that came to Conrad. Bill Thanum, the tractor dealer, is on the lead tractor. Henry, Jake, John, and LaVern all bought one, which they had ordered. They drove tractors in the parade and then right on home.

it on top of the truck. Hearing that Idaho had road weight limits, they called home for another truck. Ted Thompson and Russel Boe went to rescue them. They met at Jackpot, Nevada and transferred some of the seed to the other truck. There was about 250 bushels. It was a good variety for malting and the brewing companies would purchase all we could grow. We, our son, Don and neighbors all planted some to increase the seed. We grew it for several years. It would shell easily when ripe and better varieties of malt barley were developed which ended up replacing the Betzes.

Loretta, Charlotte, Donald and Dale all had registered seed fields. Everyone rogued to clean up the fields from weeds and wild oats. Roguing entailed walking through the fields, removing any plant that did not belong in that crop field.

Before we put in the hay field down by the Dry Fork, we put up hay on shares with Albert Leys and Frank Myers. They irrigated it; we cut and baled the hay. Vivian and Loretta were the tractor drivers on the pull type baler and two guys had to hand tie the bales with two wires. A man sat on each side of the bale chamber, one on the left side shoved two wires through and the man on the other side twisted the top wires ends together and then the bottom wire ends together. At that time wire was used, no twine bales yet until they figured out how to use the knotter system off the grain binders.

It was hot and dry working in the fields, "remember this is before cabs, air conditioning and fans. For years we used canvas water bags which kept the water cool by evaporation. I always hung mine under the seat of the rake or mower." When motorized equipment was developed, the water bag was hung in front of the radiator. Usually there was a hood ornament from which to hang it.

Fences:

We did lots of fencing. In the early days, we had to dig the postholes by hand using a posthole digger and tamp them in with a post bar. We always did fencing when the ground was wet. Usually after seeding was done, it was fencing time. Vern Flickinger, Merle Norton, and Clarence Nierenberg helped fence a lot. In the hills, I would drag the posts up the hills with the saddle horse. Many of those cedar posts are still in place now 60 years later.

It was important to watch when the railroad was replacing ties, as we used the old ones for corner posts. Then it was a chore to get them picked up and home-lots of muscle. After the floods we were able to rescue railroad ties that had washed out into our pastures. We would pull them to the truck with a lariat and saddle horses. What fun!

Another improvement was getting a three-point hitch posthole digger and a post driver. Steel posts became available after the war, I think in the 50's.

Hired Hands:

Some of the men who worked for us during the 1940s and 1950s were LaVern and Melvin Weisgram, Laurence Stoetzel, Clarence Selenski, Harold Trisco, Ted Thompson, Jason Girard, Peffer, and Don Weisgram.

Ted and Clarence Nirenberg were from North Dakota, the rest were all from Minnesota.

When we had gone on a Minnesota trip in the early 40's we had stopped to visit at Nick Hentsen's. Nick's wife was mother's bridesmaid. Harold Trisco worked for them at the time. Hearing about the availability of jobs and higher wages from LaVern and me, he gathered up three friends and they all showed up for work. That was the beginning of the Minnesota boys coming to work in our area of Montana. They were all good hard working young men. Many of these families are still in the Conrad area.

Frank Boggs came to us when Reverend McCorkle brought him from Miles City. Three generations of this family have worked for us to include Roger and Ed Boggs.

Louie Belik was with us many years. He had to go for a 3-day haircut once a month, rest up a day and be back on the job. The men always ate with us around the table. I cooked three meals a day. We did up their laundry with the wringer washing machine and dried the cloths on the outdoor cloths line. They were like family. When they brought a wife with them, she took care of her man.

There were many relatives who worked for us including Ray and Marj Heinitz, Wilber Heinitz, Larry Able, the Puzon boys, Don and Hazel Butler, and Neil Snoddy, and there are many more that I did not name.

Chapter 9
Challenges/History

Challenges and History:

Changing farming techniques:

The story of crested wheat grass:

In 1932, LaVern went to Bozeman, taking an agriculture short course, along with Glen Hollandsworth. It was for a quarter. They had a small introduction in welding, and cropping. He was aware of the blowing sandy land they farmed continually, over tilling the soil with their usual tools. He heard about crested wheat grass, a drought tolerant, dry land grass—so about 20 or 30 acres was planted by the well. Of course, saw no stand the first year. We learned later the nature of the grass, so Pops tilled it up but the grass persisted. This first patch was the seed base for many other fields. Cattle have grazed these fields successfully for 75 years. These fields are excellent for early spring grazing before the native grass grew. As years went by, more and more acres were planted on that sandy, blowing soil. First was north of the buildings, then the Morrison place, Stattler and etc.

The extension service was beginning to promote strip farming. The first strips east of the house were established.

Noble (of Canada) developed the Noble blade. The stubble stood up and held the snow and slowed run-off. Between the strips and the blade, no longer was the soil churned up and erosion stopped. Eventually all the real sandy ground was converted into crested wheat grass and the cowherd increased in numbers from 50 or 60 to 200 cows.

D6 and Noble Blade were used to break sod and cultivate stubble to help prevent blowing soil.

WWII and Army Points in 1940:

According to how many acres you farmed and the number of cattle you raised, you got so many points and could get so many hired men; we got one. They wouldn't have to go to the army. LaVern had a wife and kids and enough points, so he didn't have to go. The country needed food. Food production was a priority then.

The ration stamps came in books. Each person got a book. Things like sugar, flour, fuel and tires were rationed. When a hired man came to work, we asked him to bring some of his ration stamps, especially those for sugar.

Crops - The Big Harvest:

In 1948, we had one of the biggest crops we ever harvested. The barley made over 100 bushels per acre. We were using pull-type combines at that time. LaVern said they put the cutter bars on the ground and never saw them--prayed they'd not pick up a rock. Campana barley and Yogo winter wheat always did lie down when ripe. These two crops were the popular varieties available to us at the time. We also raised Thatcher spring wheat and mustard.

When sod was broken out, usually in the spring when the ground was moist, flax was planted first. There was a good market for flax. In fact, in the 1920's some of the flax straw and seed were processed at a flax mill in Conrad.

One day the women and kids were sitting at the new house-building site in 1948 when we heard a big snap and bang. Looking to the East across the coulee, we saw the ends of the red grainery fold out with grain spilling to the ground. We counted little kids in a hurry as they had been over there climbing up the ladder on the end of the granary and looking into that bin. They were all accounted for. We were thankful. Later, it was rebuilt, putting cribbing on the inside--no danger now.

"We were dumping a truck filled with grain from the harvest. I was driving the truck and Clarence Selenski, the hired man, was bin man. He unloaded the trucks. The bin was full, and he went up the ladder to shovel the grain a bit. Then the ends opened up. As I stood there in horror and awe I saw Clarence emerge and I was so thankful no one was hurt."--Loretta

Another incident occurred a few years later at the same red granary. Clarence discovered at the end of the day that he had lost his wallet. We looked all over outside where he could have lost it. We concluded that the only place it could be was in the bin. Sure enough, when we emptied that bin, the wallet was found.

Floods:

In June of 1948, we had a three-day rain that caused lots of flooding. The Dry Fork was bank to bank.

The water took out the road to the Marias River and the Dry Fork Bridge. Lots of railroad track was washed out. The Great Northern buses came through and had dinner at our house. Our caterpillar tractors were hired to do dirt work to repair what the floods had destroyed. Vernon Venetz (my brother) even ran one for a while.

The basement for the new house almost filled with water. What a mess. This is the reason why the big diversion dike was built to the West of the house.

After the flood, we went to check out the farm. We found pigs that had floated down from the highway bridge. A mama pig and two babies even got up to the grain field. LaVern walked down toward the river to check on a bull, who was not in the best disposition. He charged LaVern, and lucky for him, some trees were close by. He out waited the bull and came back up the hill. Of course all the audience was handing out advice.

On June 8, 1964, we experienced perhaps the worst flood ever in the area. It was even worse than a similar flood caused by similar events 16 years earlier. Tremendous rains of about 10-17 inches poured down on the snow packed watershed of the Teton and Marias Rivers. This flood washed out the dike on the east end of Lake Frances. The original Swift Dam and Two Medicine Dams broke and left paths of death and destruction 150 miles long. Numerous miles of highways and roads were destroyed, as well as several miles of railroad. It took out the highway bridge, so we had to drive or walk

1964 flood.

over the railroad track to cross the Dry Fork to get to Conrad. Thousands of head of stock was lost as well. A large area of land west of Valier was covered with water and piles of uprooted trees. Our son-in-law, Erling rode horseback with many others searching for missing bodies after the water went down. Nineteen people lost their lives.

Swift Dam was built as part of an irrigation system that was developed, on paper, in 1893. This would serve about 72,000 acres of farm and ranch lands in the vicinity of the project. Settlers or purchasers of land that was to be irrigated purchased one share for each acre they were to irrigate. Swift Dam was constructed in 1912 on Birch Creek. It is a rock fill dam with a concrete slab facing up stream and compacted earthfill on the down stream slope.

The final project was comprised of two storage reservoirs and 360 miles of canals and lateral ditches. The second storage area for water for this project was Lake Frances. These projects also provide water to local towns. Swift Dam was rebuilt and dedicated July of 1967 following the flood.

Missile Sites:

There is a missile site know as "P2" on our land. We were told about the plans for this group of missiles at a meeting at the Ledger Hall, in the 1960's. These are inter-continental ballistic missiles. Our country roads were improved and the building of the silo for P2 was very interesting. LaVern and Erling drove right into the huge hole that was made during the preparation of the silo. Many hours were spent in negotiation for the right of way as the site divided our farmland. It was not easy. We see the Air Force service members around checking and closing down these sites.

An unfortunate event would revolve around this missile site. Moe, the hired man and a few others were butchering a beef down by the corral one winter day. One of the boys with his dog had been in the corral harassing the heifers, until some finally jumped the fence to get away from the menace. The heifers went down south of the corral in a small pasture. All of a sudden, Moe saw a military helicopter coming in low over the top of the heifers, nearly hitting the power line. The heifers, of course, ran. Beauty, the horse, was also there and quite frightened. Later LaVern and I went to put the heifers back into the corral, but they were nowhere to be found. I looked over the hill to the east and there they were floating in the reservoir. About 20% of the replacement heifers had run out onto the ice covering the reservoir and the ice broke. They were unable to get out, and drowned. No way could the Air Force get out of that one, as we had witnesses to the low flying helicopter. The Air Force came right out, recovered the bodies and disposed of them. We were very angry and upset over the loss of our select replacement heifers.

The Whoop-Up Trail and Fort Conrad:

The Whoop-Up Trail connected Fort Benton, Montana through Fort Conrad to Fort McCloud, Canada. Supplies would be brought up the Missouri River as far as paddle wheel steam boats could travel, and that was where Fort Benton was built.

Then those supplies would be transported via oxen drawn wagons to Fort McCloud. Teamsters would have 12-14 oxen pulling 2-4 wagons. They would leap frog from water spring to water spring the entire 320 mile trip north to provide much needed military supplies to the Royal Canadian Mounted Police stationed there and, supplied various trading posts in the area. The supply wagons would back-haul hides, pelts and coal to Fort Benton. The boats that brought the supplies and people in to Fort Benton would return down the Missouri with hides, pelts and passengers. Military supplies for Fort McCloud were a must.

Fort Conrad was located on the northeast corner of our ranch. It was short lived and was an offshoot of Fort Shaw, a military trading post, just north of Great Falls, Montana. I think it was a military move of some kind to protect the trading post, as there was Indian activity in that area. The trail was

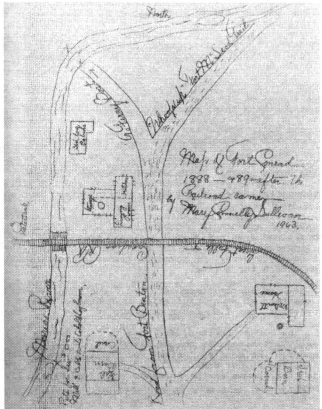

1888 - 1889 Fort Conrad map.

Vivian standing above Marias River near Fort Conrad.

the direct route from Fort Benton and Fort Conrad and was a good location to cross the Marias River. In high water, the teamsters could use a ferry to assist with crossing, and in the winter the river could be crossed because the river would be frozen over with ice. When the river was low, the teamsters could cross with no assistance. Remember, in those times horses and oxen were used to move all of the goods.

The Fort Conrad trading post was there for many years. James Willard Schultz lived there, ran the trading post with his wife, and wrote a good story of that time. He loved this country.

At one time, there were plans to draw an irrigation ditch out of the Dry Fork and irrigate some of the flat land around the Fort Conrad trading post. They were going to really go into pig production. The plan was to drive the pigs overland to Fort Benton when they were ready for market. A flood ruined the irrigation ditch and the building of the railroad ended that project.

We still have a bit of the irrigation ditch. It is just south of the apple train wreck curve.

When the trading post closed, all of the buildings were torn down and hauled off, as lumber was a scarce resource. We got the old railroad tie icehouse and used it for a few years.

We have enjoyed going down to that area and finding artifacts such as square nails and dish fragments. We have even dug through their old garbage dump to learn more about those that passed through and those that lived there.

Lots of family picnics were held there as well as in later years, Farmer's Union get togethers and so forth. There are still a couple of basement holes you might drive into, as Everett Grigsby did once.

About 1963, the historical society from Cut Bank placed a Whoop-Up trail historical marker there near the railroad bridge. We had a big gathering there for the event. It rained while we were there, and when our son Dale was headed up the hills out of the valley, he slid off the road. We had to go up the hills by the old sod way up next to the hogback to get us all back out. Those who had come from the north for the event had walked across on the railroad bridge to get there for the event.

We always enjoyed a walk across the bridge but watched out for the trains. Some people dived off that bridge into the river for fun. There was good fishing in that river as well. Although I did not marry a fisherman, my parents enjoyed that sport.

In 1964, a flood tore out the east end of the bridge and a lot of the railroad track in the area. LaVern went down and pulled the Whoop-Up Trail marker back from the bank as it nearly was washed into the river.

A few years after that someone stole the historical brass marker and the cattle rubbed the concrete base down. We now have a new marker, and it will be put in the trading post area on our side of the railroad tracks.

The Whoop-Up Trail was no longer needed when the Canadians finished their transcontinental railroad in 1880 and could get supplies to their police forces. Additionally in the United States when the narrow gage railroad was finished between Great Falls and Lethbridge, it was yet another way to move supplies.

The trail was always an important piece of history for this area, and we commemorate it annually. We now have the Whoop-Up parade and rodeo every spring in Conrad. The Ledger women's Club always had a float in the parade. On one Ledger Club float, some of the gals wore corsets on a nicely decorated float. Another time they all wore big cowboy hats.

We had one Indian float with some of us in Indian dresses and got Frank Boggs to dress up in an Indian outfit and be on the float. Another year the float was themed as panning for gold. We threw little rocks out to the crowd. Yet another year we had an old toilet on a float with me sitting on the hole with a Montgomery Ward catalog, as they had been used for toilet paper, as we did not have toilet paper at that time. We also put together a historical float showing the rivers, roads and Whoop-Up Trail. It was a fun time getting together to do up floats.

We would haul horses to town for the girls to be in the parade. It was always a busy time.

Now we just go and watch the parade and if it is nice, we also go to the rodeo. LaVern always thinks they make the best hamburgers there at the rodeo.

In 2000 and 2001, a group called Due North was going to conduct a wagon train that retraced the old Whoop-Up Trail from Fort Benton to Fort Macleod.

In 2000, they went from Fort Benton to the Montana-Canadian border where the trail crosses the no man's land and enters Canada 8 miles west of Sweet Grass. This location is marked by a wonderful monument.

In 2001, the wagon train met up on the Canadian side of the border at Coutts to continue the journey to Fort MacLeod. Charlotte was in charge of the last 60 miles in Montana for the 2000 portion of the wagon train, because she was familiar with the area having been raised and had a farm in the area. She was key in procuring permission from landowners to cross their land or have a camp on their land. The wagon train followed the trail as closely as possible.

Many times we were *on* the actual trail, as the ruts are still visible. Many participants were consumed with the historic feeling of what it must have been like

Monument marking the Whoop-Up trail, crossing between Montana and Alberta, Canada.

"on the trail." Daily historic news letters would highlight events of long ago for that days trek.

Every so often, they would encounter a large rock W inside a rock circle. In 1964/65, some Boy Scout groups had emplaced these symbols while retracing this

Rocks in the formation of a circle with W marking the trail.

historic trail. They were able to erect two monuments and 17 markers on the trail from the Marias River to the Canadian border.

Charlotte and her daughter Gwen each drove rebuilt 1800's spring wagons on the entire trail. Loretta, Jennifer, Don's daughter, and Jennifer's daughters Kylie and Katie Schlepp also rode in the wagons or rode horses during this event. When the wagon train arrived on our place, we gave them a tour of the Fort Conrad area and showed them where the crossing was located. One of the trees in that location still shows the scars from the ropes that were used to ferry across people, wagons and supplies. The wagon train had to cross the river using the current highway bridge (F bridge) as the water was too high to ford and the railroad prevented access. The outriders from the wagon train came down on the north side and got to look at the tree that the ferry tied up to. That wagon train averaged about 20 miles a day.

Fort Conrad also served as a training site for the military on occasion in the more recent times. The Shelby National Guard unit would come out to the Fort Conrad site, train for common tasks such as map reading and markmanship, and conduct maneuvers for several years. Charlotte's husband, Bob, and her sons, Clay and Ward were part of that unit at the time. They came with their tanks, trucks and other equipment and would camp and train.

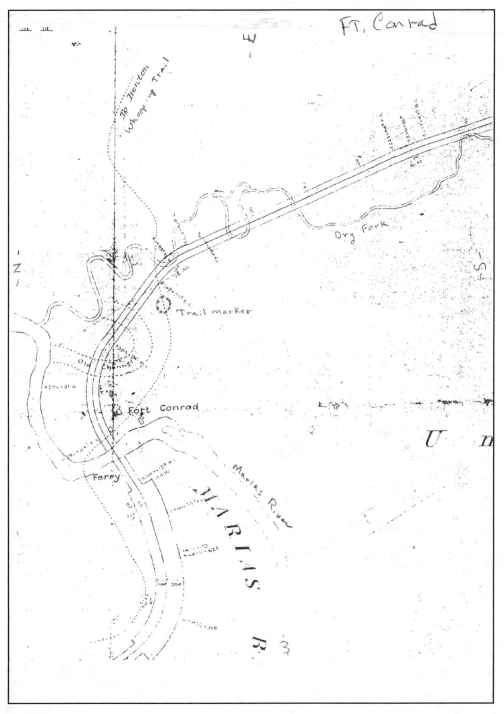

Fort Conrad

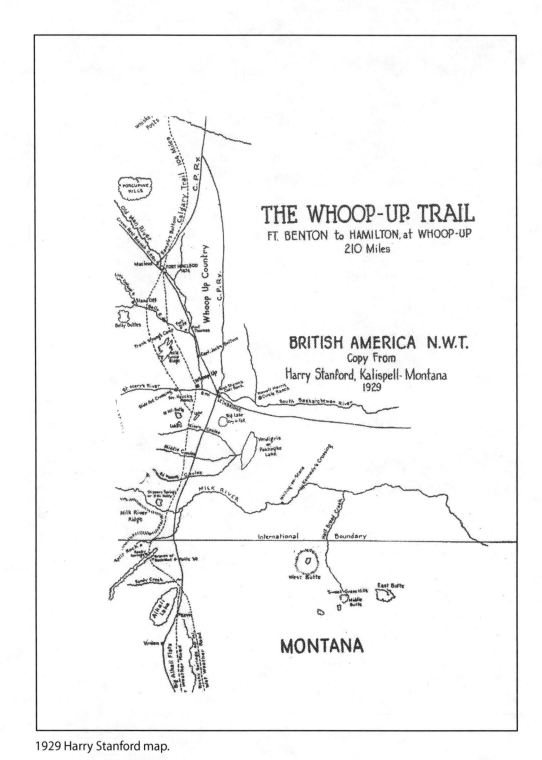

1929 Harry Stanford map.

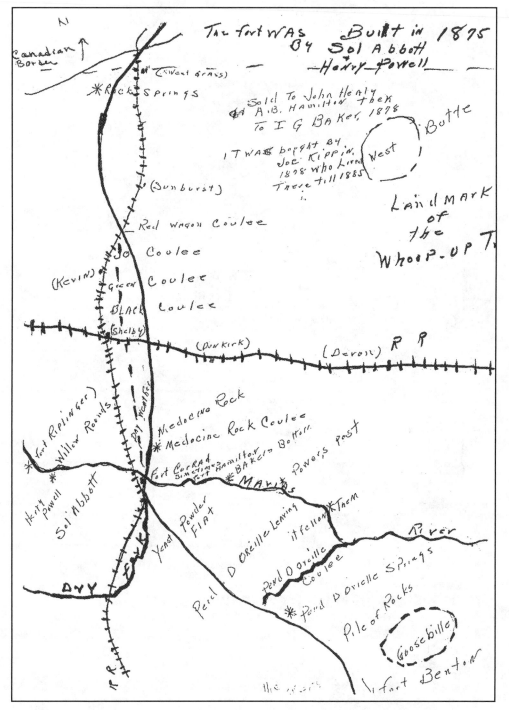

Whoop-Up Trail fom Fort Benton to Canadian border.

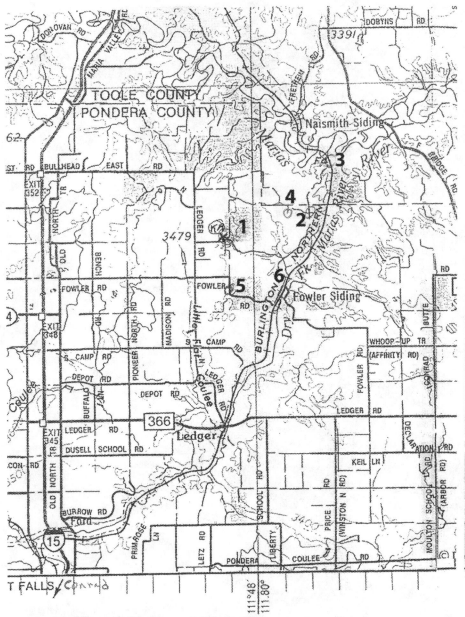

1 - Keil Ranch (LaVern & Vivian Homestead)
2 - East Place
3 - Apple Train Wreck
4 - Bum Ridge School
5 - Fowler School
6 - Fowler Siding is also Town site

Chapter 10
People

Presbyterians:

In 1919 when Moms and Pops worked at the hospital,. Moms cooked and Pops was the janitor. LaVern, Leviene and Calie went in to spend Christmas with them. Moms sent them down to the Presbyterian Church for Sunday school. When LaVern went into Conrad for high school, he stayed with Mr. and Mrs. Craig. She was the organist for the Presbyterian Church so she took LaVern along for services and upon occasion, he would pump the organ for her. In fact when Joey Fowler and Bill Judish got married, LaVern was the organ pumper. At their 50th anniversary, LaVern was honored for having performed at the wedding. This is how LaVern become involved with the Presbyterian Church.

When I came to high school, I stayed with Mrs. Berkland. She took me to the Presbyterian Church and got me involved with the youth group. Having no church involvement before that, it was a learning experience for me. The pastor was Reverend McCorkle and he would come out in the country to hold church services at schoolhouses. This way, he could keep in close contact with his parishioners. Reverend McCorkle married LaVern and me and baptized all four children. He always raised a great big garden, giving vegetables to anyone in need.

LaVern served on the Presbyterian Church session, the governing board of the church, and was a trustee. I was a trustee, deacon, and session member. I traveled to the National Presbyterian meeting in Michigan and Texas. During this trip, I met missionaries and many interesting people.

LaVern and Everett Elliot were chosen by the Presbyterian Church to attend the National Presbyterian Church men's fellowship meeting in San Francisco. Helen and I accompanied our husbands as they drove many miles. Some of the topics of conversation included was Lee Harvey Oswald guilty, where to stop and who was paying for meals and gas. We had such a good time, such fun, to travel with good friends.

The new church building was built and the Presbyterian camp at Flathead Lake was a project we both supported.

4-H:

When Loretta was 10, the Ledger Cooperative's 4-H Club was started. So, that was another iron in the fire in our lives. The meetings, projects and camps kept us busy. LaVern and I were 4-H club leaders and put in 4 years on the state's 4-H Council. We were chaperones to the 4-H camps for many years. When our 4-H Club was disbanded, our family had put in 64 years of 4-H Club work.

We sold many calves to 4-H club kids, and they placed well, many getting blue ribbons at the Shelby Fair and the Great Falls Fair. The club girls did sewing and cooking projects as well.

We chaperoned kids at the 4-H camps. I conducted the handicraft classes. LaVern was in charge of the hikers. Dale caught a little fish in the creek and the cook cooked it for him.

Farmers Union:

In the early years, 20's and 30's, the Farmers Union and family groups had picnics down near the railroad bridge over the Marias River. It was really a nice place under the trees. They had baseball games as well as doing a bit of fishing. Where the Dry Fork ran into the Marias River was a really good fishing hole. If making ice cream, they stuck the freezer crank into the Model T wheel and let it churn the freezer.

Leslie, Gus, Henry, John, & Alice Keil Venetz at picnic making ice cream; by hooking ice cream maker to the spoke of Model T.

Many people had to back the Model T cars up the Marias hill. It was too steep to go forwards up the hill. Model T's had no fuel pump so the tank had to be higher than the engine.

In the 1940s and 1950s, we were active in the Farmers Union activities. We were leaders in the youth groups, going to training sessions and camps. One time, it was at the abandoned schoolhouse by the Price place. I was one of the chaperones. The boys slept in the barn and the girls in the house, and we cooked in the schoolhouse. One day, Aunt Norma Keil brought over 40 chickens and we had the kids cleaning them. Yeah, now, they raised a lot of

Rising Sun campgrounds. Farmers Union camp.

chickens and she sold them. She just brought them down to the camp and put the kids to work. What a feather fight they had. Then the cooks prepared a wonderful chicken dinner for all. Yum! We also camped at the Rising Sun Camp Grounds in Glacier Park for three years. LaVern and Chief, (our Saint Bernard dog) guarded the cook tent and led the campers off on their hikes.

In the 30's there were Farmers Union picnics at the F-Bridge. We rode horse back down. There were also baseball games.

LaVern enjoyed being on the Farmers State Bank board of directors. This was one of his favorite accomplishments. We had the opportunity to attend many state bank meetings, including one at the Big Sky resort.

We were active in the Cattlemen's Association and I still enjoy membership with the Cowbells, the women's branch of the Cattlemen's Association.

Chapter 11
Tours

Soil Conservation Tours:

We had many wonderful experiences while LaVern was on the Pondera County Soil Conservation Committee. One trip we took was to a ranch at Platte, Nebraska where we toured the Ogallala Aquifer seeing crops and water development. We learned of the water table being lowered because of wells, this in turn caused them to have to drill the wells deeper. We saw the grand sand dunes created during the 1930 drought. When we got on the plane to leave, the window fell into my lap. Needless to say, we got a little bit excited and it was fixed before we took off.

We took a trip to San Diego, California by bus with Dale and Sheri and boys to observe farming techniques there. It had been raining hard for several days and the farmers had been trying to harvest their vegetable crops. Several roads were closed due to mudslides. At one farm, they were pulling the broccoli-harvesting machine with extra Caterpillars. Many fields were underwater.

During a trip to Florida, we observed the takeover of waterways by agriculture, and the use of oyster shells for graveling roads. Here we saw the harvesting of lettuce and other vegetables and the processing of those crops clear through to the bagging of salad mix for McDonald's.

Ranch Tours:

We toured many cattle operations in the Houston, Texas area. We saw the feeders, cattle being prepared for slaughter, and the uses of the by-products, including manure.

Another tour was to the Yucatan in Southern Mexico by bus. Here we saw the Mayan ruins and a ranch with Brahma cattle. These cattle were taken to shows in Spain. Their beautiful hair was like velvet. We saw abandoned fields, shanty houses, many skinny dogs and naked children. They were very poor. The President had just been there, so the area had really been cleaned up. The seashore was beautiful white sand. At the hotel, they locked up our passports and anything of value whenever we left the hotel and kept the key at the desk. Even going to the pool required us to secure all of our belongings. We met the Jelks on the tour and later visited their ranch south of Tucson, Arizona right on the Mexican border, a couple of times. The elevation there was 3000 feet and they received thirteen inches of rain, so it was by no means desert country. He was an electrical engineer and had a fascinating rock and mineral collection.

In Florida, we visited the big Mormon ranch, the John Deere memorial gardens, and went out on a night dinner-boat ride up and down the coast for several hours. It was wonderful to see the lights on the coast as we sailed along.

Loretta and Erling went along to Phoenix, Arizona to the National Cattlemen's convention. Our tour guide was Basque, the vice president of the Arizona Cattlemen's Association. We saw the feed yards south of Phoenix by the Mexican border. They were utilizing the waste carrots and lettuce from California. There were some very thin cattle from Mexico. They grazed the harvested fields of all kinds of fruit and vegetables controlling the cattle with electric fences. They used lots of maze and corn. One big problem they had was birds feeding on the huge piles of grain. They could not shoot the birds because it would contaminate the grain, so they installed machines that made big banging noises like a gun shot. The ranchers got several cuttings of alfalfa a year since they have a longer growing season and milder temperatures. Brahma cattle are popular as they can stand the heat better. They sweat and cool themselves with their large ears. We traveled west towards Yuma, and back through the mining area in northern Arizona.

We also visited Nashville, Tennessee with Loretta and Erling. During that ranch tour, we toured southern Kentucky and Chattanooga, Tennessee. We saw horses being trained to high step for showing. The tails were trained and chains put on their feet to get the hi-step. We saw a new computerized cattle sales ring, a first for us. All of the cattle came in small lots and were sorted according to condition and size and brought into the ring in large lots.

In the 90's we traveled with Taylor Brown, an agriculture commentator, on a feeder tour to Oklahoma and Texas. Having met a lady on our Australia tour we stopped in to renew a friendship with her `on our trip to Texas, also saw the L. B. J. Home, big cattle feeding operations in New Mexico, toured Indian ruins, the caves up on the mountain, and on to Arizona.

Another Cattlemen trip with Loretta and Erling took us back to California. We made a circle north of San Diego and the Salton Sea, crossing over into Slovenia, a Dutch town. Here they were making hay cubes by compressing small hay bales and making them a foot long for shipment over seas. At the big dairy we observed the care of small dairy calves and the modern milking parlors.

Twice we went to the Sieban Ranch out of Helena to the Democratic rally for Max Baucus. His father owned the ranch. LaVern had met Mr. Baucus on a soil conservation tour to Mandan, North Dakota. We became very good friends, meeting often at state conservation meetings. Max has been a friend and we were always welcome to his office when we were in Washington, D.C. His interest in solving problems in Montana agriculture made him a valuable spokesman for Montana farmers and ranchers. Mr. Baucus was a staunch Republican and said of Max, who turned Democrat upon going to college in Missoula, Montana, "well he did come out alright". Often Max has done a lot of work on sheep grazing on federal lands, keeping the cost per head down; not a Republican sponsored program.

People-to-People Tours:

We were able to take many trips. First overseas one was with the People-to-People program. These were farm-oriented trips. We were to be ambassadors. A group of 36 went for 30 days to Belgium, Denmark, Netherlands, Russia, Hungary and Germany.

In Netherlands, we got to visit with Ove Staun and wife. Ove was an exchange student who had been our guest.

Again, with People-to-People, we went to South America to Uruguay, Paraguay, Brazil, Argentina, and Peru. Calie and Moms were with. All our tours were agriculture oriented. Got to see people building roads with wheelbarrows and shovels. They could have used tractors, but they were giving people employment. We also watched cattle sales, grazing practices, and some of the work exchange students were doing.

We went on a tour to Australia, New Zealand, Tahiti and Maui, Hawaii. Alice and Vernon were with us this time. We saw bananas growing, Wineries, panda bear reserve, sail boat competitions at Sidney, lots of sheep ranches, and the aborigines—poor and otherwise.

The second time to Australia and New Zealand with Taylor Brown, we went to Brisbane, Sidney where LaVern climbed Ayers Rock and Perth was where the sail boat races were held. This time we got to do bed and breakfast at three different ranches—one sheep, one dairy, the other agriculture.

Chapter 12
Family Trips

Family Trips:

In 1949 or 1950, we took a trip to see Moms and Pops at Tucson, Arizona in January. We went on down into Mexico to Guaymas, about 200 miles south. We went out fishing one day. Chartering a boat with all the riggings, Mr. Emrick and Mr. Banka came along. Donald caught the first fish. You can imagine his alarm when his fish was used for bait. Poor kid. We went on out 25 miles or so to an island and watched the porpoise and seals play. A bunch of whales came up around our boat and really scared our guide, who had been sleeping on top of the cabin and not watching, and us too. We caught a couple big fish. We gave the heads to the Mexicans who used them to make fish soup. Loretta got seasick and didn't enjoy the trip. We spent one day in the desert hunting arrowheads and the group found some real nice ones. They would be lying on top of the sand. We were careful to put a flag on the car antenna so everyone could find their way back. Back in Arizona, we went to car races, out to all the orchards, then on up to Phoenix to see the Salad Bowl Parade. It had snowed in Tucson so everyone was out making snowmen.

Often when we would visit Moms and Pops in Arizona, we would cross over the border into Mexico at San Louis. Pops and LaVern always got their shoes shined so they could pay the little kids. One time an older boy took the money from the little boy who had just shined their shoes, making the young boy cry. He told one of us that he could

Lavern and Charlotte hiking at Glacier National Park to Ptarmigan Tunnel.

not get home now with no money. We gave him money so he could smile again. To this day, there are still shoe shine boys and the folks that wear shoes that can be shined.

We made several trips to Glacier National Park and enjoyed family hikes.

We traveled twice to Alaska, the first time was with a tour, and the second was with Earl and Arlyce Feda. We spent time with their son Billie Feda on Kodiak and went out fishing—caught halibut and salmon.

We made many trips to Arizona after 1941 as Moms and Pops stayed winters there, went down several routes to see lots of western U.S. We traveled many times to Minnesota to visit my relatives and on to Kansas to Keil family reunions.

In the winter of 1942, LaVern, Loretta and I took a trip to Kansas to visit relatives and friends. Among them were Aunt Hannah and Phillip Foos and many of the Keil's.

"While the folks and Loretta were gone, Donald and I stayed with Grammy and Grampy Venetz at their ranch S.W. of Conrad. One of our special treats I remember was a glass of cold milk with homemade bread chunks in it and a spoon of sugar on top. I would spend hours looking out the window, waiting for the travelers to come home."--Charlotte

After visiting in Kansas, LaVern, Loretta and I drove to Missouri and visited Victor and Minnie Ray. Victor had worked for us and we wanted to visit him. The party line ring alerted Minnie's neighbors "the new company had come." Minnie fired the stove with corncobs gathered from the pigpen. When we needed to go to the toilet, we had to use the chicken house. There was no toilet or toilet paper. We had to wash our clothes when we left there. We gathered corncobs from the yard after the pigs had cleaned them off as "toilet paper" and fuel for the stove. Later the Ray's came to Montana as a family to work for us.

From Missouri we went up through Iowa to Minnesota. Here we visited mother Venetz's family. We did all kinds of things together. One day while visiting a relative, there were no toys for little girls so Loretta was given some old greeting cards, paste and she had a great time. We went to visit cousins, it was so cold and the wind blew so hard it seemed that it could blow in one crack and out another. Everyone sat around in lots of clothes. One night we drove about 40 miles to a dance. Lawrence Welk was the band that we danced to.

While at Albert and Toots Hedke's place, Loretta got to feed the big kitty with a baby bottle. They milked about 10 cows.

One of our trips to the South (Arizona), we left Dale home with Katie,

Even the kitty got milk. Loretta feeding the kitty at Hedke's in Minnesota.

the hired gal and her boyfriend who did the chores. She became the cook for the summer. When spring work started, she was still my cook. There were lots of cookies and so on—she had the freezer so full, Dale had to stop her. When the men came and left from breakfast, she met them at the door with lunch boxes and if they forgot them—tough luck. She was the ruler of the roost.

Many of our trips were with Alice and Vernon Venetz. We would call about a proposed trip and their bags would be packed. They were great traveling companions and we could go way back to our dating days; good times.

We spent several winters at Quartzite, Arizona in Donald's RV at Ray and Marj Heinitz's yard. Lots of the family camped there including Erling and Loretta. It was a great gathering place for all the friends and relatives to stop. Ray and Marj were great hosts. Large groups of us would go out to the desert. We had to return on Friday night for fish at Sweet Darlenes. The other evenings we would enjoy potlucks and camp music around the fire. I do remember though that during one of our visits to the South, we got caught in a blizzard in Wells, Nevada.

Switzerland:

In 1982, LaVern and I, Bob and Charlotte (Keil) Marshall, and Erling and Loretta (Keil) Grubb made a memorable trip to Switzerland to seek and see Matt Venetz's, my dad's, childhood home. His family lived in the town of Reid near Brig. We drove to Bretten, parked the car and took overnight bags up the mountain tram to the Reideralp Arthur Farar Hotel.

When the Venetz family was there, they drove the cows up to Reideralp from Reid each summer. The cattle grazed and were milked on the mountain. The cheese was packed down to Reid to sell. We stayed in the hotel and reflected on Grandpa's stories of selling Edelweiss flowers to the tourists.

We saw cows with the huge bells around their necks and a man packing a huge milk can on his back down the mountain. It was an unbelievable, emotional and wondrous trip. We visited the home Grandpa lived in until he was five.

The original Venetz home was still there and had been built in 1759.

We hiked down the mountain from Reider Alp to Reid.

We saw the village church where some Venetz records are. We had lunch in the village and rode the tram back up the mountain to the hotel. We also took a guided tour of many points of interest in Switzerland.

Venetz home in Switzerland.

We were so enthused to be able to experience the beautiful Swiss countryside. We stopped the cars to hear the cow bells ringing on the hillsides. There were different sized bells on the cows, making a nice melody as they grazed the mountain side.

What a great event to find the original Venetz home still there, as it is now gone. It was wondrous to see the glaciers, mountains, villages, and the cows we had heard about. What memories we have! And now, we share them with you.

Village of Reid, Switzerland where Grandpa Venetz's home was along with the old church steeple. Venetz family records are still at the church.

Epilogue

Here we are, at the ranch. We have seen another harvest finish and now it is time to move the cows onto the stubble.

We celebrated our 74th wedding anniversary here in our home and shop. Old friends, neighbors and relatives came. We had such fun visiting and remembering old times. We received so many wonderful cards and notes recounting Farmers Union Camp, 4-H Camp, and many other activities. It was a wonderful journey.

Vivian Venetz Keil and her husband, LaVern Keil have remained on the ranch for over 75 years.

She has riden and driven horses thousand of miles and cooked thousands of meals (delicious). She has cheered on her children, grand children and relatives. She has been a true partner to her husband. Her home has welcomed all who came through the door. She is the epitomy of the pioneer spirit!

And our kids:

Erling and Loretta help on their ranch and love to enjoy the grand children and great grand child. Bob and Charlotte build horse drawn buggies and wagons, enjoy their farm, and their mountain get away near Essex. Don is busy managing his Sanfoin seed business, from the field to seed sales. Dale and Pat commute between the Keil ranch and the law office.

Blessings to each reader

This moving history chronicles families immigrating to America in search of the American dream, hoping for a better life. Farm families came from Russia and Switzerland in hopes of realizing the awesome opportunities advertized, "land for the taking" if you could homestead and prove up on it. These families had perilous journeys and unbelievable obstacles on a daily basis, but back then, it was just a way of life. Their journeys bring them all to the rugged frontiers of northern Montana. Vivian recounts the homesteader era hardships, adventures and triumphs along the way. The reader gets a firsthand farm and ranch perspective of the taming and settling of this part of the country. These were pioneers of their era, tough as nails with unquestionable work ethics. They were all a part of a truly great generation that made immeasurable sacrifices without question for the good of all. We will never get to experience their spirit or vigor except through stories such as this that have been captured.